A BLOCK OF TIME

a time to learn, a time to grow

By

WILLIAM SCHMITZER

Contents

Prologue

I began writing a military and Vietnam War memoir for my children when they were young. Should I die, they would never know what their father saw and experienced. I also felt because of the Vietnam War, the United States would never engage in another conventional war. Since this was going to be our last war, I wanted to document my service for history's sake.

I found it wasn't too difficult to write about these experiences since they were stamped or imprinted in my mind. I wanted my children to see and feel what I felt and saw. I worked on it for years, slowly writing down one experience after another. By then the children were in their teenage years, and I was now a firefighter with the Orlando Fire Department. After years with the department, I started writing again. What started as a memoir intended to document two years of military service, now incorporated a career with the fire department and a move from Florida to Tennessee.

I was, at first, apprehensive about the idea of publishing, but I decided that the historical importance alone was valuable enough to get my story done and in the hands of family, and anyone else who cares to read it. After working on it, I find myself wanting to encourage everyone to write a memoir—it will be valuable to someone and serve as a historical document of whatever time and era you have lived in.

I began the memoir by writing in cursive on notebook paper. I've been told I have nice handwriting, but after a while it became illegible. Plus, having to erase or draw a line through a sentence made it worse.

Because of a learning disability it was often difficult to get my thoughts on paper in a way that flowed. Spelling has always been a weakness for me, so before computers and cell phones I would have to use a thick red Webster dictionary to look up words. Even then, it was frustrating as words starting with vowels were often difficult—I didn't know which vowel it started with—I'd sometimes have to go through each vowel before finding the correct word.

I was fortunate to come of age during the personal computer and cellular phone era. In the 1990s, I moved everything over to a personal computer, and the Google search engine, once it became available, helped me immensely with my spelling. I was glad I'd taken typing in high school.

I'm concerned I might have elaborated too much or gone into too much detail. This may be true, but I'm fortunate to have the ability to remember the smallest details, and I consider what I've put down to be important for history's sake. For example, I understand some readers wouldn't know, or care, what a "Halligan bar" is, or what it's used for, but it's important to the history of the Orlando Fire Department.

I often wished I had photographs of what I saw, those split-second images that are stamped in the forefront of my mind. I can still vividly see the Vietnamese mother and daughter in close embrace. The expressionless faces of war prisoners, the young boy's face when I returned his Christmas puppy to him, and Jim Reynolds' concerned expression as he closed the ambulance door—a picture has a way of expressing thoughts and emotions that words cannot.

Military Service and
the Vietnam War

In 1968, I graduated from Edgewater High School with a general diploma that took me thirteen years to complete. In elementary school I was told I was a slow learner, and there may be some truth to that. It was blamed on my likely exposure to lead paint when I was a toddler. It affected my ability to read, spell, and comprehend, making it hard for me to keep up. So, with grades of low C and D I knew college, at that time, wasn't for me. I was taught to work diligently with my hands and that became beneficial in the future.

My father served during World War II as an aircraft mechanic stationed in North Africa. Since my father was small in stature, the US Army initially trained him as a machine gunner on a B17 bomber—he would fit nicely in the tail gunner position. When he was diagnosed with colorblindness, he was put to use elsewhere. Being good with his hands and able to fix just about anything, he was reassigned to a position repairing aircraft. Both of my uncles on my mother's side volunteered to become paratroopers. My Uncle Bill, my mother's twin, was a combat engineer with the 101st Airborne and experienced combat during Operation Market Garden and at the Battle of the Bulge. Uncle Roy, Mom's younger brother, served in the 82nd Airborne and was heading to the Pacific theatre when the Japanese surrendered. We clearly had a family tradition of serving our country.

. . .

My best friend in high school was Larry. He, like my father, was short in stature, yet agile and fit. He was also funny, energetic, and somewhat of a prankster. My mom and dad enjoyed when he came to visit, as Larry had a way of making them laugh. We were the same age and had common interests. I respected him for his ability to figure things out and for his knowledge of mechanical things. He completely rebuilt the engine of his 1950 Ford in his parents' garage. Graduating a year ahead of me due to my learning issues as a youngster, he enrolled at Seminole Community College where he took classes part-time and worked part-time. Because his parents couldn't afford to help with tuition, he relied on his income from his job at the *Orlando Sentinel* or, as we called it, "the paper."

Larry was instrumental at getting me a job with him in the mailroom at the paper when I was a senior. On my first night of work, Wednesday evening, I saw my eighth grade math teacher readying himself for work. Even at that young age I knew teachers didn't receive adequate pay and some worked part-time. To think about it now, it's sad; he would work until 12:00 or 1:00 a.m., drive home, get a few hours of sleep, then be back at school at 7:00 a.m.. This additional burden of having to work not only affected his physical health and well-being but possibly the learning of his students. I was a little uncomfortable seeing him there, as I liked him—he was a good teacher.

The mailroom was a large open-floor building sandwiched between two press rooms. The main newspaper—front page, local news, and sports page—were printed on gigantic rolls of white newsprint paper in the press rooms. From there they were sent on conveyor belts to the mailroom where additional supplements were added or inserted into them, such as the parade magazine and sale flyers. Larry and I along with about ten college students worked at either the inserting machines—inserting publications into the main newspaper—or bailing and stacking bundles of newspapers. We worked Wednesday nights from 6:00 p.m. to around midnight or sometimes later. On the weekend we worked from Friday evening at 6:00 p.m. to around 5:00 a.m. in the morning. If we wanted to work Saturday, and Larry and I always did, we could return around 7:00 a.m. and load the trucks with the bundles of the Sunday edition. We worked until all the trucks were loaded at mid-day. It was long, continuous work, but we were in good shape, and we received fairly good pay at the time.

. . .

Shortly after I graduated, I received my draft notice. Larry, because he couldn't afford to attend college full-time, also received his notice. We both boarded a Greyhound bus and sat side by side for the two-and-a-half-hour ride to Jacksonville, Florida, where we would receive a full physical examination. We both passed and in less than a month would be sitting once again side by side on a Greyhound bus, this time heading to Fort Benning, Georgia.

The morning I was to leave I woke early; I had to be at the bus station at 7:00 a.m. My mother knew I was anxious when I refused breakfast. She loved me and was concerned because her twin brother, Bill, who I was honored to be named after, was killed during the Battle of the Bulge. Years later she shared her concerns about my going to war, telling me I was so much like Uncle Bill and didn't want anything to happen to me.

When we arrived at Fort Benning, it was around midnight; I was told later that all new recruits arrived in the late hours of the night. I think we remained in the reception area for two to three days and, in that time, were given haircuts, dog tags, uniforms, vaccine shots, and a small pocket Bible. The army also gave us a small cardboard box where I packed my civilian clothes and shoes to be mailed to my parents back home in Orlando. We also filled out a lot of paperwork, including forms about our work experience and others related to life insurance.

One afternoon we were marched into a building to have our teeth checked by a group of dentists. Before the examination, they gave us a toothbrush with a small dab of fluoride toothpaste and a paper cup of water. We were told to brush for a specific amount of time then take the water into our mouths swish it around and spit it back into the cup. I did as asked and spit the white frothy toothpaste in the cup. I happened to turn to the fellow beside me and as he spit a mouthful of bloody yellow and brown toothpaste into his cup, I almost threw up.

At the reception station area, we were treated fairly nicely. There was probably a reason for the kindness as was our nighttime arrival, but the kindness and pleasantries were going to come to an end. We were lined up and loaded onto olive drab school buses then driven to where we would undergo basic training. This is when Larry and I had to part ways. I would find out later that Larry would go on to volunteer for the infantry and then attend Non-Commissioned Officer school. Afterwards he was sent to Vietnam where he would lose both his legs from a landmine. I am sad to say I only saw him two times after we both returned from Vietnam. On our first visit he made me laugh when he said he asked the doctor to make him taller by making his prosthetic legs longer. The doctor said he unfortunately could not because it would affect his balance. He was able to walk with the help of forearm crutches and, at times, a wheelchair. The very last time I saw him he had just bought a Ford van and was having it converted to make it accessible for him to drive. We lost touch soon after free-spirited Larry headed to California. Years later, soon after the Vietnam War memorial was dedicated, I saw him pictured on the cover of *National Geographic* magazine standing on top of the memorial while a bugler played "Taps." After even more time had passed, I received unfortunate news: Larry had taken his life. Deeply saddened, I wished we had stayed in touch. I've tried for years to obtain more information about how Larry got to that point but have been unsuccessful. On the bus bound for basic training that day, I sat beside the person in front of me in line resting our duffle bag on our laps. I don't remember how heavy the duffle bag was, but I would soon find out. It seems to me we rode for a while before we got to our company area. I didn't know where I was, only that I was assigned to "E" company (Echo Company) at Sand Hill. I know why they called it Sand Hill because our company area was somewhat hilly, white sand everywhere along with short needle pine trees. I never saw any of that red Georgia clay.

As the bus stopped, army life became real. A large, gruff, muscular E-6 (staff) drill sergeant stepped up into the well in the front of the bus and said, "You better not be the last one off." It was then mass chaos, guys struggling to not be the last one; luckily, I wasn't, but the poor soul that was, was told to do a thousand push-ups. I didn't think anyone could do a thousand push-ups, and I'm sure he didn't, but the fear was planted. The numerous drill sergeants started spouting orders using every obscenity known to man. We lined up in five rows of ten, and with our duffel bags held high over our heads, we ran from one end of the formation area to the other. I can't find words now to describe the depth of the fear; I only remember thinking, "Boy, did I make a mistake!" But what choice did I have? I just hung in there, did what I was told, and tried to do my best, so, hopefully, I could graduate. If you didn't graduate in the eight weeks you would be recycled through once again, and I certainly didn't want that!

I don't remember how many drill sergeants were assigned to our barracks but there were two that stood out. One was an E-6, probably a career soldier. He was a big man in his early thirties, though looked much older. On his olive-green fatigue shirt, he wore the Combat Infantryman Badge (or CIB). One afternoon, during a forced march, I overheard him telling a colleague that he had been shot on his last tour of duty. He certainly could have been the poster boy for the army with his cropped haircut, starched fatigues, and boots shined to a mirror finish. He was the kind of soldier I would follow.

The second drill sergeant, holding the rank of E-5, was tall and slim. He didn't fit the image of the career soldier, at least in my mind. He had also done a tour as an infantryman in Vietnam, and I overheard him telling of a battle during which he used an M79 grenade launcher to keep the enemy at bay. He liked me for some reason, and on the weekends, he'd call me out of formation to man the phones in the orderly room while he took the company on a run or march. When called, I'd quickly run to the orderly room, hoping the phone wouldn't ring, and it never did, not once. I was thankful. As much as I felt uncomfortable overseeing the orderly room and its responsibilities, I appreciated not having to go on the long runs, as they were usually grueling, especially when *he* took us out.

Every morning before daybreak we were signaled by a loudspeaker to exit our barracks. We were to run and shout to our respective formation areas. If we didn't run fast enough or shout loud enough it was back up the hill to our barracks to do it again. One morning we performed this exhausting routine four times. By the end of our fourth attempt, we were so exhausted the drill sergeants gave up.

After inspection of the troops, it was off for a run. We never knew the distance nor the route, so we had to pace ourselves and hope we didn't fall too far behind. Once back at our company area we were given about twenty minutes to rest and use the latrine. We were then marched to the mess hall for breakfast, but before entering we had to navigate the horizontal ladder. We had to jump up, grab the first rung, and hand over hand work our way to the other end next to the mess hall entrance. At the start of training, I was barely able to complete the task, but, in time, my hands became calloused, and my strength greatly improved. After finishing the ladder, you recited your service number, the same number that was on your dog tags. My number began with the letters US, which indicated I was a draftee. If they were RA, it meant you had volunteered; NG or ER signified you were in a national guard or army reserve unit. The drill sergeants verbally abused the NG and ER soldiers.

I personally liked mess hall food. I was usually hungry when mealtime came, and if I remember correctly, we could take as much food as we wished, but we had to eat it *all*. If we were at the rifle range during the midday meal the mess hall would bring our food to us. We ate off of metal trays, and after the meal it was our responsibility to wash the trays. Two large, heavy metal cans, resembling trash cans, were filled with water and placed over a propane fire. One can was filled to the top with scalding, soapy water; the other, also scalding, was clean rinse water. So, being careful, we first dropped our utensils into the soapy water and then, holding the edge of the tray, you scrubbed it with a long handle wooden brush. Once it was clean, you dipped it a couple of times in the clean boiling water then stacked it on a portable table.

A "basic training day" was always filled with activities, such as learning how to march, field classes, practicing at the rifle range, and, of course, a lot of physical training (PT), and long runs. We each had a web belt—secured to the back was a canteen of water and a poncho. We wore only the helmet liner and not the steel pot you see in old photographs of the war. When we did PT or went on a run, we took off our web belt, helmet, and long-sleeve fatigue shirt and neatly stacked them to US Army specifications. We did our PT and ran in black leather combat boots—no tennis shoes or shorts were permitted in the army at that time. After PT or a run, we had about a minute to get our shirts on and tucked in, our web belts secure, and our helmets on. Just putting on the heavy cotton long-sleeve shirt was always a problem for me due to my excess perspiration. More than once, I had a bulge of shirt tail material between my belt and hip making for a most uncomfortable feeling. And if you happen to get your boxer shorts involved in your haste this could also cause chafing between your legs, but we put up with it until we had a chance to rearrange ourselves.

We marched or jogged everywhere. No trucks or buses. We often sang cadence led by the drill sergeants. A few have stuck in my mind even after all these years. "I want to be an airborne ranger, I want to live the life of danger, all the way, every day," was one. And "river of Saigon, river of Saigon, oh bloody river" was another. There were some that were perverted, filled with profanity. I was never one to use profanity—a junior high English teacher of mine told the class that when we use cuss words, we are showing how ignorant we are. This stuck with me throughout my life, though I really was quite ignorant. Every other word that came from the mouths of our drill sergeants was profane. One particular drill sergeant who enjoyed making us do push-ups would say, as we sweated and grunted on the ground, "Knock 'em out, god****it! Knock 'em out!" My father used profanity, though my mother never did, but even Dad would never use the word "god****it" or "son of a b****."

The rifle we were each issued—the army called it "your weapon," was the M14. I was told that though the M16 was now being used in Vietnam, the manufacturers couldn't keep up with the demand. So we used the old, reliable M14. It was a very solid, accurate, high-powered rifle. It shot a heavier bullet than the M16 did, and the gun itself was heavier in weight. When we marched with our weapons, we placed it on our right shoulder and held the buttstock with our right hand for support. This was called "right shoulder arms." But we often had to run or jog with the rifle held in front of us diagonal across our body with the barrel pointing slightly up and to our left, this was called "port arms." Running and holding the rifle in front of us was exhausting especially after miles of running.

I did enjoy the rifle range. My father was an excellent instinctive shooter and I guess some of that rubbed off on me. One morning I was lying in the prone position firing at a target about 50 yards away. I grouped three shots very close together. I didn't notice the company captain watching me shoot until he leaned down and said, "Nice shooting, Son." His complimentary tone was sincere and encouraging, and boosted my confidence. I don't remember any names of my fellow soldiers or drill sergeants. I only remember being in the company of different races, young men with different levels of education, many with levels lower than mine. They came from different parts of the country, and some, it was easy to see, were poor. Some wet the bed at night. Some had no concept of how to function, but I think in time, most of those not fitting the army mold were given a general discharge and sent home. As I put in my time, as I watched, learned, and listened, I suspected many of these soon-to-be soldiers would have a difficult time adjusting to army life, especially if they were sent to fight as infantry soldiers in South Vietnam.

Sundays, after our morning run, we were "off duty," so to speak. Most of the troops left the company area, leaving the area peaceful and quiet, relative to the constant activity. I never left the company area except to attend church. I always looked forward to the service. I chose not to attend the Catholic service though I grew up attending the Catholic church. There was something about the Catholic mass that didn't resonate with me. The army chaplains did offer a Baptist and Methodist service, both of which I sometimes attended. I found them peaceful with a sense of goodness, a couple hours of reprieve from learning how to fight, kill, and destroy. After church I'd go to the mess hall for lunch, then back to the barracks for maybe a nap or to write a letter home.

All the barracks, at least from what I saw, were constructed in much the same way, dating back, I'd guess, to World War II, or maybe even before. The one I was housed in stood two stories and was constructed of wood. They were built on top of brick piers, if I remember correctly, and because of the company area being somewhat hilly, the front portion was off the ground maybe 4 feet and the back maybe 2 feet, so the structure was level. It was heated with chunks of black coal that gave off a distinct odor I oddly found somewhat pleasant.

Immediately after entering—you entered on the right side through a simple screen door (the inner wooden door seemed to stay open all the time)—the latrine was to your left and a few steps farther were the stairs to the second floor. I was somewhat uncomfortable with the latrine layout. There were no walls or partitions between the six or eight toilets lined up against the wall, and no individual urinals, just a trough, or gutter-type device, that you walked up to, stood shoulder to shoulder with the guy next to you, and urinated. There was no privacy at all, and the urinal trough could smell quite bad when four or five troops went at the same time. The shower area was one big, open room with shower heads extending out from three walls, similar to the showers in gym class.

At the top of the stairs was an open room that mirrored the first floor, with two rows of bunk beds from one end to the other. My bed was an upper bunk about halfway down on the right. On the far end of the structure was another wooden door inside and a screen door, which served as our back door and led to a small porch with stairs that descended to ground level. Sometimes I'd sit on the open-door threshold to write letters home, rest my feet on the porch. Close by were short needle pine trees that I felt were nicer than the long needle pines in Orlando, and I liked their aroma on a breezy day. Moments like this were important—peaceful time alone with myself, the trees, and pen and paper. Because our barracks was definitely a firetrap, we had fire watch throughout the night. This involved having a rotating schedule in which one person stayed awake and alert throughout the night.

Having even brief memorable connections with the other trainees on a personable level were just as important as solo time. One Sunday after lunch, heading upstairs for a nap, I reached the top where there was a small bedroom to the left, directly over the latrine. I usually never paid attention because the door was always closed, but this afternoon a soldier was sitting on the bed with one pant leg rolled up to his knee. He turned to me in the doorway and said hello. I returned the greeting. I noticed his freshly starched kaki uniform hanging from a wall locker. The E-5 sergeant stripes were creased in half from the starch. I also noticed a few award ribbons in a neat straight line on his shirt. I only recognize one ribbon: the purple heart. My Uncle Bill had been awarded this metal after his death during

World War II. Above the ribbons was a badge with a rifle laying across a wreath. At the time I didn't know what it represented, but I had noticed that all the drill instructors had them sewn on their fatigues. I would later learn it was the combat infantryman's badge, or CIB for short. Yet I was quite certain he wasn't a drill sergeant; he was too pleasant. I don't remember how we got on the subject of his exposed leg but as I looked closer, he pointed out small pieces of shrapnel lodged under his skin. He was actually removing a few with tweezers. It didn't look painful necessarily, or in the least way unsightly. He said the deeper pieces were surgically removed but the ones just under the skin would eventually come to the surface like a splinter. I wish I would have had the maturity and forthrightness to ask more questions, about him, about this war that was going on in Vietnam. I can't help but wonder how this veteran is doing today: Is he struggling with his physical wounds, or with PTSD, or both? I only remember him as being nice and willing to take the time to say hi and talk. That meant a lot to me since I was lonely and far from home.

On the last day of our training, our company huddled around the entrance to our platoon barracks. We listened to our now quite nice, respectful, and funny drill sergeants as they read out our military occupational specialty number (a.k.a. MOS) and where we would be stationed next. I would say 98 percent of our platoon was assigned an infantry MOS number and sent to Fort Polk, Louisiana, for advanced infantry training. I was one of the few assigned a number other than infantry.

Apparently, the occupation form I had filled out stating I knew how to cut meat was noticed by the army. I had learned this trade from my father who owned a butcher shop. So my next duty station would be Fort Jackson, South Carolina, to work with primarily civilian meat cutters providing meat for the large basic training facility. I was given a leave but don't remember for how long. I also don't remember what airport I was sent to for my first ever airplane ride. Though I do remember a young boy, maybe ten or eleven years old, who was accompanied by his mother, sat next to me on the plane. He had flown before; I was the newbie in my kaki uniform with one stripe sewn on the short sleeves.

I reported to Fort Jackson on a Friday afternoon. Where I encountered a lone E-4 clerk. The first thing he said was, "You know you didn't have to report until Monday morning, right?" He knew by my appearance I was fresh out of basic trading and didn't know the ropes. He was nice, however, maybe even felt a bit sorry for me. He was able to find an empty barracks for me to stay in until Monday when I would officially report for duty.

The area was depressing and with no one around I felt lonely and homesick. I went to a pay phone and called my parents collect. My mother picked up the phone and the operator said she had a collect call from Bill Schmitzer and asked if she would accept the charge. She said yes, and my father got on the other extension. It was so good to hear their voices, but I soon broke down and started to cry. They didn't have to ask if there was a problem. Mom knew I was just scared and lonely, as she knew me well. I couldn't hold back my tears, crying for the first time in front of my father, something I would never do for fear of his response. But I think he understood and both of them did their best to comfort me. I felt better after I cried. I wonder now if soldiers had been around, would I have had the strength to hold it in? As I look back, I see how I was a grown young man, learning to be a rough and tumble soldier, yet frail and weak at that instant. I'm not ashamed to write about crying. I've only cried a few times in my life due to emotions, yet those times did release that pent-up feeling, emotions that only a good hard cry can accomplish.

. . .

Monday morning, when I officially reported, I was given living accommodations in a nice, clean concrete block multistory barracks. This barracks housed the different tradesmen, including meat cutters and bakers, who were to provide food for this large facility with its numerous mess halls.

My cubicle mate was Rick, he was from Hattiesburg, Mississippi, and he also had just graduated from basic training. Rick was quite ambitious and found a part-time job at night pumping gas at a station just off post. This small, southern, two-pump gas station still provided personal automotive service. An attendant would come to your car, pump your gas, check the oil and tires, and clean the windshield. Rick was like Larry, very mechanically inclined.

Our first day of work at the meat processing facility was to "work the rail." This rail, or track, was suspended above the floor about 7½ feet and ran throughout the facility. This is how the beef was moved or rolled from one location to another.

Our job that first morning was to meet the tractor trailers delivering the beef and veal. These new and clean trucks would arrive with their refrigeration units (or "reefers") keeping the beef cool and fresh. Before the rear doors could be open, the military food inspector had to be present. The inspector would first check the temperature inside the trailer, and if it wasn't within the appropriate range, the whole load could be rejected—quite costly for the shipper. Because they wouldn't want to lose such a lucrative contract, the beef was usually shipped in newer more reliable trailers.

After we were given a white cotton coat and apron, we would take turns lifting the quartered beef off the hooks in the trailer and rehanging them on our rolling hooks. Once secured, the beef was easily rolled down the rail into the large cooler room where it would stay until it was ready to be cut up. From there, either eight front quarters or eight rear quarters were rolled into the cutting room where it would be broken down into smaller more manageable sections. These sections were placed on large stainless steel tables were the civilian and military meat cutters would cut them into roasts, steaks, stew meat, etc. All cuts were separated and placed into heavy aluminum rectangular pans with one handle attached to to the long end. Approximately 16" x 20" and 6 inches deep, these pans, when full, would be placed side by side on a rolling cart and wheeled into the walk-in freezer, where they were kept in the freezer until it was time for them to be delivered to the mess halls.

I worked the rail and cutting tables for a little over a month. I was then assigned to work in the delivery section, a job I more or less enjoyed. We got to work outdoors and, since it was the fall and early winter in South Carolina, it was pleasant. My duties were to load a short wheelbase tractor trailer with the pans of meat and, with the assigned driver, deliver them to the mess halls. My driver was an African American in his forties. He was tall and slim, always neatly dressed in matching trousers and a long-sleeve button-down shirt. He was also extremely thorough with safety always in mind. Every morning, he would arrive in an army green, single-axle tractor and back under my trailer. After securing the trailer, he would turn on the refrigeration unit to start cooling the trailer, and check the trailer lights.

Our duties were to drive a designated route to each mess hall. The driver would stop at the rear of the mess hall and beep his horn to alert the mess hall staff there was a delivery. I would stand at the back door of the trailer and when the kitchen help arrived, I'd pass down their tagged pans filled with meat. When finished and with all personnel clear, I would push a small button attached to the trailer wall twice, sending a signal to the driver to proceed to the next mess hall. After all deliveries were made, I would climb up in the warm cab for the ride back to the plant. I liked my driver. We would talk but I don't remember ever talking about anything of substance. What a missed opportunity to have a conversation with a black man who grew up in the Deep South at that time.

Rick bought a 1947 Dodge refurbished pickup truck from his boss. It looked good and ran well. One cool pleasant Saturday we decided to drive west from Fort Jackson toward the Appalachian Mountains. After breakfast, we drove out the west gate, through the city of Columbia, and were soon on Interstate Highway 26 heading towards Asheville, North Carolina.

We never made it to Asheville because at some point we exited the interstate and started driving two-lane county roads. These roads made sharp hairpin turns to the left and then to the right. We were now definitely climbing and enjoying every turn and overlook. As we continued to climb, the air temperature dropped. We were excited, as this was our first visit to the mountains, and these were somewhat cold temperatures for southern boys. Rick's old Dodge did fine, though to help with the climb he did have to downshift the three-speed transmission shifter attached to the steering wheel column. We rounded one sharp curve and on Rick's side of the road we saw a patch of white. I said to Rick, "Is that snow?" It was just a small patch that apparently the sun's warm rays weren't able to reach to melt. We pulled over to see snow close up for our first time seeing snow. I instinctively reached down, grabbed a handful, made a snowball, and threw it at Rick. I'm sure we looked silly playing in such a small patch of snow.

Hopping back in the truck, we continued our journey, our adventure down the narrow two-lane roads. We enjoyed hiking some short trails, gazing over beautiful forests, and experiencing the aroma of different smells. We stopped at a small rural gas station and country store for gas and got something to eat. It was one of those days I'll never forget. The temperature was cool and mild with a low humidity. The cloudless sky was so blue. I had never before seen a sky that clear and blue. It was beautiful. As late afternoon rolled around, we felt it was time to head back. We got directions back to I-26 and headed east.

About an hour away from Fort Jackson, in the dark, we got a flat tire. We pulled off to the shoulder of the road, and Rick informed me he didn't have a spare. We noticed an exit not far up the road, so we removed the right rear tire and took turns carrying it to the exit. At the exit we looked right and saw a town marker and headed that way. I was a little scared and told Rick I had a pocketknife if we had any trouble. I don't think Rick was concerned; he was more accustomed to rural living as opposed to me growing up in the city.

I don't remember us walking too far from the exit when we came to the small community. The first structure we encountered was a small gas station on the left side of the road. One lone African American man was working. I believe it was his station and, based on the few folks I saw, it seemed to be a mostly African American community. The man, dressed in a well-worn pair of bib overalls, appeared to be in his fifties with strong arms and a thick upper body. He rolled our tire over to a tub of water and inflated it. He didn't have to submerge it because under the light he noticed a nail in the tire, and we could all hear the air slowly escaping. He took the tire off the rim using a manual tire changer, pulled the tube out, and put a patch on it. He then carefully placed the tube back in the tire and reinstalled the tire, being careful not to pinch the tube. He then added air, rolled it back over to the tub of water, and checked for leaks. I don't remember much conversation between us white boys and this gentle black man. He asked if we could pay three dollars for the repairs and Rick said yes. Rick gave him three dollars and the kind soul took the tire to his old wrecker truck placed the tire next to the boom that extended out the back and told us to hop in. Rick didn't hesitate so I climbed in and sat next to him.

He drove us to the exit where we thanked him, then lifted the tire from his truck, and carried it up the ramp and down the shoulder to

Rick's truck. After snugging up the lug nuts, we headed home. As I sat there staring straight ahead, I thought of the kind soft-spoken man who went out of his way to help us. This was my first interaction with a black man, a race my father disliked. But this man was kind and thoughtful, how could anyone dislike or disrespect him? As I now reflect at age seventy-one, I can honestly say I love that man and truly respect him. He touched my heart. I saw a decency in him that few men possess. I stayed in South Carolina for about four months before I received orders for Vietnam. One sad problem we had at the South Carolina fort was the terrible race relations. Living in Orlando, I wasn't aware of any race problems, but I was definitely ignorant at that time. At the Fort there were often threats or fights between African Americans and whites. I stayed to myself and tried to use good common sense. One Saturday morning as I descended the interior stairwell, I encountered three African Americans ascending. We met face to face, and I'm sure my eyes told them I was scared. They stared at me, and me at them, with my descent blocked I felt they were deciding what they wanted to do, but then their faces changed. No words were exchanged; they parted and let me descend. I believe they could have hurt me badly, but they knew I wasn't a threat, and I held no animosity towards them. That encounter scared me, and I sensed there was a much deeper problem between races than I knew.

. . .

I received orders for Vietnam and was given, I think, a two-week leave. I was to report to Fort Lewis in Washington state. I flew into the Seattle-Tacoma airport and took a bus for the 26-mile ride to the fort. The one thing I remember on my bus ride was how large and tall the evergreen trees were out the window. I had never seen trees this massive. Once at the fort, I was placed with hundreds of other soldiers and issued jungle fatigues and combat boots. The boots were leather, but the sides were a nylon mesh. I was told a metal plate was in the sole of the boot to provide some protection from *punji* sticks. A punji sticks, or stakes, were a type of booby trap. Numerous sticks were sharpened at one end and stuck in the ground or a hole and camouflaged. If a soldier stepped or fell on these stakes, they would most likely be pierced by the extremely sharp points, causing lacerations or puncture wounds. We were also told that poison was sometimes applied to the points. I had never seen a punji trap but understand they were very painful and debilitating if encountered.

We boarded a large commercial airliner and took off early one morning. Our first stop was in Alaska. Upon landing there were large mounds of snow everywhere. We had to disembark and walk across a large open area to a terminal. Our tropical fatigues did little to keep us warm from this extreme cold. Luckily, our walk wasn't a long distance. I think we made a few other stops for fuel, but after about twenty or so hours of flight we landed in the late afternoon at Cam Ranh Bay, South Vietnam.

From Cam Ranh Bay, the army sent me south, from one unit to another, trying to place a soldier with a meat cutter MOS. At a layover at Bien Hoa, I had an opportunity to visit some Vietnamese merchants. One merchant took portrait photographs of soldiers to be sent home to parents, wives, or girlfriends. I scanned the photographs hoping to see my friend Larry. At that time, I had no idea what his MOS was, or his location. I did happen to see a photograph of one of my basic training comrades. He, like most of our platoon, were sent to Fort Polk, Louisiana, for advanced infantry training (AIT). I pointed to the framed 8 x10 photo and said, "Do you know him?" The Vietnamese gentleman said in his broken English, "He dead. He died." I was saddened and just stared at the picture. He most likely arrived in country soon after AIT, and his unit was assigned to this area. There I was, standing before him in my new stiff olive-green fatigues. In the photograph, his fatigues were faded and somewhat frayed around the collar. He would be the only member of our platoon that I'd come to know the fate of.

•   •   •

I finally ended up at the 335th Assault Helicopter Company, the "Cowboys," in the Mekong Delta. I was assigned to first platoon, the "Ramrods," as a helicopter door gunner. I would have to learn this on the job, since I knew nothing about being either a helicopter crew member or about the workings of the M60 machine gun. I was issued three flame-resistant Nomex flight suits, gloves, flight helmet, flak vest, and two M60 machine guns. Jon, my crew chief, was an excellent teacher, explaining what my duties were in and around the helicopter. Now when it came to the M60s, I was just plain ignorant. I even had to ask another door gunner how to load the gun. Luckily for me and my crew members, my first few flights were uneventful and when the guns had to be fired, it was only to spray a tree line that was probably not a threat. The guns often jammed, and this was a big concern for me since it was my responsibility that the guns operated at all times.

My other duties as a door gunner were to secure the blades when the helicopter was "shutdown" for the night. If the blades weren't tied down, the wind or rotor wash from other helicopters could cause the blades to flop up and down and possibly damage them or their connection to the rotor hub. My other duties were to operate the refueling nozzle. When we needed to fuel up, we would hover over and land beside the "POL" area, meaning petroleum, oil, and lubricant. The hose and nozzle were quite large in diameter in order to fuel as quickly as possible. With the turbo jet engine still producing power to the rotor blades, I would open the fuel tank cap and fill the fuel cells. The crew chief would always be close by if needed or to man the fire extinguisher if we had a fire. We could also obtain ammunition from this area. Another duty I had was to clean the floor when we returned to base at the end of our missions. This could be as simple as removing most of the spent cartridges from our machine guns, or it could be more time consuming, having to scrub the floor to remove mud and/ or dried blood.

I was fortunate to not only have Jon as a knowledgeable and caring crew chief, but to have also met a door gunner from another platoon who was "short," meaning he was due to return to the states in a week or so. While he was still there, he took the time to help me understand this gun. I don't remember his name, but he had been awarded the Silver Star Medal for heroism. Apparently, his helicopter was extracting troops from a "hot" landing zone, and he dismounted the helicopter to rescue an infantry soldier who was down and wounded. One evening we met after I came in from a flight. He told me to take the guns and clean them, and he would meet me at my barracks after he had supper.

The gun cleaning area was a small wooden shelter with a metal roof and open sides. A single low-wattage light bulb with a pull chain illuminated the area. Dangling from one post was a "no smoking" sign. On each of the two 8-foot long tables were 55-gallon metal drum cut in half lengthwise and secured on their sides. Each half was filled with a mixture of JP4 jet fuel and motor oil. (I never considered looking closer at the drums. They could have been discarded containers that once transported the herbicide and defoliant we referred to as Agent Orange. Our area of operation was heavily sprayed, and I saw the effects, but never knew of its hazards to humans until years after I came home). I disassembled each gun and thoroughly cleaned each part making sure no part was lost or left in the drum. I secured all the small parts in a towel and walked back to my cubicle. I then took a clean, olive drab bath towel and laid it over my footlocker, then completely drying each part, I laid them on the towel.

When my friend arrived, we sat on the edge of my bunk. In front of us lay one of my machine guns. He then said, "Let's scope on this." I still use this same expression today when I want to understand something or explain something to someone. I told him I had some knowledge about how the M14 rifle and an automatic shotgun worked. I felt the M60 worked on the same principle. He agreed but added because the M60's ammunition was belt fed into the gun there are more moving parts to heat up, weaken, and break. By the time class was over, I felt I had learned a great deal about the gun: I could visualize in my mind every moving part and how they worked together, from when the trigger was pulled to the bullet leaving the barrel, the empty cartridge being ejected, and a new live round seated into the chamber. At nineteen years old this was the first time I felt I really knew or understood something of importance. I don't want to sound proud or arrogant, I'm only saying it was my responsibility to the helicopter crew members that the machine guns preformed their job, just as the pilots and crew chief were responsible for performing their respective jobs for all of us. From that day forward, I never had any major problems with my guns. If one became inoperative in flight, I had additional parts to get it promptly back in service.

Though getting machine-gun parts was difficult, I didn't fully understand why until years after I came home. I read an article about the president of South Vietnam during the time I was in country. It reported on how corrupt he was and how he sold American arms and ammunition on the black market. I had also heard that munitions were stolen and sold by American soldiers, but I didn't want to believe that (though I'm afraid it may have been true). I thought the shortage of machine gun parts was due to the overall complexity of war, and it was oftentimes hard for parts to trickle down to the company level. The two machine guns issued to me were quite worn; I accepted that and did not expect to be issued new guns. I went back to the company arms room to request parts, but the sergeant said he could rarely get any. This was a frustration, because I knew I would need some replacement parts, especially those parts that were most prone to fail. I didn't need a full barrel bag of parts (a barrel bag was a heavily constructed, flat, zippered canvas and nylon bag used to keep the parts secured). I figured three sets of barrels and matching bolts would be nice, plus any parts I could acquire to keep the guns ready at all times.

There was one part that broke the most: a tiny flat piece of metal that pivoted with the help of a very small, yet stiff, spring. It was attached to the front side of the bolt. Its purpose was to grab and hold the cartridge while it was seated in the chamber. When the firing pin activated the cartridge, the bolt was forced back, ejecting the spent cartridge and seating a live round. This small part—I think it was called the extractor pin— would heat up and usually fail by splitting in half. I don't know if maybe there was a batch of these extractor pins that were defective, maybe made with inferior metal. I know it could fail, even if it was a healthy pin, if the gun was fired too long without interruption. It was best to fire in short bursts of maybe ten or fifteen rounds, letting the gun cool somewhat. This small part was very hard to change in the field and probably impossible in flight. I got fairly good at replacing it on my footlocker but had to concentrate. If the spring got away, it was gone; I rarely found it after it flew. My mission was to obtain these valuable parts. If I had a gun break in flight, I wanted to have it back in service as quickly as possible.

I had heard there was a large armory at Long Binh, about 20 miles from our basecamp, Bearcat. I mentioned it to Jon, my crew chief, and he asked our platoon sergeant if we could borrow the platoon's flight line truck. He gave us permission, and the very next day we headed out. The road was considered secure, though I was a little uneasy at first. Four of us loaded up in the old 1950s Dodge Power Wagon. The two senior crew chiefs rode up front in the cab, and another crew chief and I sat on the two bench seats under a heavy rolled-up canvas tarp that covered the pickup bed. We headed out of the gate and passed a rubber plantation on our right then made a turn onto Highway15 that took us to Long Binh. I remember passing crude structures and homes built by the Vietnamese using discarded American material. Numerous structures were made from cardboard, metal roofing, and any other material that could be scrounged by the poor Vietnamese at the military dump. How could those cardboard houses hold up to the rain? Though I would say military grade cardboard was much thicker and stronger than cardboard of today, as well as water repellent. My first country ride was an eye-opener. I was used to seeing grass huts from the helicopter, but to see these structures and the terrible living conditions made the grass hut look appealing.

We pulled up to the main gate at Long Binh, and the MPs (military police) asked our business. The driver told him we were going to the armory for machine gun parts and the PX (post exchange). He told us to wait and had us pull over. The MP sergeant asked us to take two nurses to the hospital ward. It would have been a long walk plus they had luggage. I could tell they had just arrived in country by their new, stiff, olive drab fatigues. Even though I was still fairly new in country, my fatigues were showing signs of fading, making me feel somewhat like a veteran. The nurses held the rank of lieutenant, and each had a black bar sewn on her collar. I didn't have to salute them since we were in a combat zone. They placed their gear in the back of the truck, climbed up, and sat next to us. They were nice, friendly, and enthusiastic. I believe they wanted to contribute their skills and compassion for those under their care. I remember talking with them but don't remember what about. When we reached the hospital, they climbed down and thanked us for the ride. I admired them and their sacrifice, hoping they had a safe tour of duty.

The driver then dropped me off at the armory. I jumped down, walked a few paces and opened a screen door. As I entered, I saw a soldier at the counter having a heated conversation with the E6 supply sergeant. This can be a problem, because if you get on the wrong side of a supply sergeant, you won't get anything. After the soldier stomped off, I humbly walked up to the counter. I never wore my rank so I think that may have helped; he would think I was a private. I was correct in assuming the sergeant needed to feel that his contribution to the war was important, so I asked in a way that made him feel needed and important. A supply sergeant wasn't considered a glamorous position, but I felt he and other noncombat jobs were important to the overall success of this war.

I expressed to him my problem and concerns with my guns and hoped he could help. My request for parts was sincere, and I felt he knew that. He, in turn, honored my requests and helped me out tremendously. He liked me, and when I returned a second and third time, he not only gave me the parts I needed, but he also gave me, what I would call, luxury items. I learned a valuable lesson at age nineteen treat people with respect and you'll most likely receive a cordial response.

Having these parts contributed to saving lives one morning. This day we were assigned to fly a "single ship" mission, meaning we weren't in a flight with other helicopters. We were to insert two American advisors into an open scrub area deep in the Mekong Delta. I thought this was strange because they wore civilian clothing, and didn't have a pack or water, only a 45-caliber pistol on their belt and, luckily, a radio.

Usually, with these types of missions, the areas we flew to were supposed to be secure. We dropped the advisors off and, within a few minutes, they came under fire from an enemy bunker about 75 yards from their location. I'm surprised we didn't take fire coming in or leaving. This place was so remote and such a hostile environment; I pitied anyone having to fight there. They quickly radioed us about their situation. We immediately returned and tried to rescue them but were unable due to the small arms fire. The pilot radioed for assistance as we circled counterclockwise. I moved to the left side of the aircraft next to the crew chief, Ron Pate, and we both fired at the well-hidden bunker. We couldn't penetrate the bunker, but if we could keep them pinned down long enough for help to arrive, we could rescue the advisors. As we circled, we continued firing, and my machine gun was the first to break. I quickly replaced the barrel and bolt and was back in service. Shortly there after, Ron's gun also became inoperative, so I gave him mine while I quickly got his back in service. A helicopter gunship arrived on the scene and fired rockets into the bunker, destroying it. We quickly descended to rescue the advisors.

As we came to a hover a few feet off the ground, they dove through the opening landing on the floor. Because of the hundreds of spent cartridge casings, they practically rolled completely through and out the other side of the helicopter. We finally returned the advisors to their base of operation. They were very thankful. I never learned what that situation was all about—we just follow orders.

. . .

I hadn't been in country too long, and one night, asleep on my bunk, I was woken by the bed shaking. Though I had never experienced an earthquake, I felt this had to be one. I looked over at Jon and said earthquake, he replied, "B52 strike." I was relieved it wasn't an earthquake, but it was still a little unsettling to feel the ground vibration and items on our makeshift shelf falling to the concrete floor. It seemed to last for minutes, never gaining strength, just a mild shaking of the earth. It stopped as suddenly as it started, and I fell back to sleep. I personally didn't experience another B52 strike, but they were happening. I had later learned they were prepping the area right over the South Vietnam border just inside the country of Cambodia for our upcoming invasion in May. We were only about 50 to 60 miles from the Parrots Beak, referring to the southeast boarder of Cambodia and Vietnam. It was one of the numerous exit points into South Vietnam from the Ho Chi Minh trail.

. . .

One evening, Jon informed me that the next morning, the company was to gather for a formation. This wasn't a uniform or shiny-boot inspection; it was for promotions, as well as awards, such as Air Medals, Bronze Stars and Silver Stars, Purple Hearts, etc.

Early the next morning as we started to gather, we heard a couple of explosions towards the southern end of our base, near the motor pool area. I could see some troops pointing westward, beyond the berm and cleared bulldozed area, just inside a tree line. From my fairly close vantage point, I could see a wisp of smoke hanging in the humid air. It wasn't long before I noticed a lone F-4 Phantom fighter jet heading our way. In the clear sky, I recognized it as the F-4 from its wing design, though this was the first time I saw one in flight. Streaking downward from my left to right, the pilot was lining up his target. Within seconds, the roar of this aircraft was upon us and from under his fuselage he released one napalm canister. This cylindrical canister is filled with a gasoline gel mixture, so when it comes in contact with the ground this mixture ignites and spreads forward and outward. For a brief moment, the eastern sun glistened off the cylinder as it tumbled downward. When the bomb made contact with the ground, the pilot had already started his steep skyward angle. Just the roar of the jet engines and the speed of acceleration sent a pridefulness throughout my body. I just witnessed the United States military superiority; no one should mess with us. Patriotism isn't a bad feeling—I believe we all have felt this way at one time or another when seeing and experiencing such might—but now, fifty plus years later, I feel a sense of sadness for having such feeling. This war could and should have been avoided. The volume of deaths and injury is beyond measure.

. . .

On March 31, we were woken by our platoon sergeant around 5:00am. After dressing in our Nomex flight suits, we went to the mess hall for breakfast, gathered a box of C rations for lunch, and returned to our barracks for the rest of our equipment. Jon, my crew chief, gathered his flight helmet, flak vest, and toolbox. I too secured my flight helmet, flak vest, two M60 machine guns, a Puma hunting knife my father sent me, and a barrel bag filled with extra machine gun parts.

It was still dark when we and other crews loaded ourselves and equipment in the back of an old military Dodge one-ton truck and headed off to the flight line.

On arrival, the truck driver drove slowly from one helicopter to the next, dropping off the crew members. The pilots arrived the same way on their platoon truck. The crew chief, pilot, and copilot, inspected the helicopter from nose to tail rotor, looking for any problems. My duties were to check and secure the machine guns and make sure there was adequate ammunition. Once everything was checked and secured, I untied the strap that secured the rotor blades to the tail section. With the blades free the pilots began the process of cranking the helicopter and checking the radios.

The helicopter I was assigned to was a Bell 1968 UH-1H Iroquois (nicknamed "Huey"). Our call sign was "Cowboy 384" and was considered one of the strongest helicopters in the fleet. I'd overheard pilots' comments about how they liked to fly 384; apparently she had power and handled well, and mechanically we never had any major problems. That's why we were surprised that morning when the pilot noticed a warning light indicating a problem with the tail rotor.

Our mission that day was to insert infantry soldiers into an area of Kien Hoa province on the Mekong Delta. Cowboy 384 was to fly lead helicopter in a string of six or maybe more. Three UH-1B helicopter gunships escorted us, and a command helicopter directed the operation. The pilot notified the commander of our situation with the possible tail rotor problem, and he advised us to hold fast, have maintenance check it out, and allow the second helicopter in the flight to move up to lead.

This second helicopter carried Kimball, the door gunner/crew chief who took me under his wing to show me around the company area when I arrived. Kimball was a door gunner but was taking classes from my crew chief Jon to become a crew chief himself. So, that day he was riding in the crew chief position. He had only been in the country a month before I arrived, but he sensed my uncertainty and went out of his way to make my transition as easy as possible. We both were from Florida and, not surprisingly, became friends.

With time now being a factor in the mission, the commander decided to take the flight, minus 384, and proceed to the pick up zone where the infantry soldiers would be picked up. Maintenance responded quickly, checked out our situation, and determined the tail rotor was fine; the problem was in the warning light indicator switch. A new one was installed, and we took off about thirty minutes after the main flight. We knew we would not arrive in time for the first insertion of troops and were directed to land at the pick up zone and participate in the next lift. As we were flying in, we heard over the radio that contact was made with enemy forces and one helicopter was down due to being struck by an RPG (rocket propelled grenade). We were immediately called in to assist. The downed helicopter was the one that took our place as lead. The only thing recognizable of the destroyed helicopter was part of the tail section; the rest of the aircraft was smoldering, pungent, black smoke. An infantry officer came up to our aircraft and reported that there were three wounded and eleven dead—ten infantry and the crew chief. The three wounded crew members were transported to a medical facility by another helicopter in the flight. We were ordered to transport the dead to the morgue at the medical facility. As the ten infantry soldiers were carefully being stacked on top of each other, the consequences of war were not but inches from me. My friend Kimball was still in the burning aircraft; I knew it would only be a matter of time before we would be coming back for him.

By then it was about 9:00 a.m., and the heat of the day was building as was my pain and heartache. As the last soldier was loaded, their blood and bodily fluids mixed with burnt skin covered the rough aluminum floor, oozing over the open sides of the helicopter. We took off and headed to the medical facility; the pilot called ahead to inform them of our arrival time and situation. Upon landing, a flatbed truck met us, and the bodies were unloaded onto the bed of the truck, yet to lay them on the searing hot steel of that truck seemed inhumane. With the rotor blades still turning, the pilot slowly pulled up on the collective handle and we lifted off, back to retrieve our brother in arms, my friend.

As we made our descent to the scorched ground, an infantry soldier activated a green smoke canister to indicate where he wanted us to land. As we sat down, I noticed on the crew chief's side of the helicopter an object lying on a heavy plastic poncho. I knew this was the body of Kimball. Three infantry soldiers pulled the corners of the poncho together and slid Kimball's remains across the dried bloody floor. Once again, up we went to make another flight to the medical facility. As we banked slightly right, I turned my head to the left and looked again at Kimball's body. With the ends of the poncho flapping in the wind I hoped his death was quick, but I couldn't know that. It was around noon when we banked to the left and started to descend. I saw an army ambulance heading to the flight line to meet us. Kimball's remains were unloaded, placed on a stretcher, and slid onto the floor of the ambulance. As the ambulance drove away, I heard 384's engine winding down. It would be a few minutes until the blades came to rest, and it was time to secure them with a hook that had a thin nylon strap attached. This hook inserted into an eyelet on the outer ends of the blades, making it possible to walk the blades around until they were in line with the aircraft; the strap was then tied to the tail section.

The pilots told us to stay with the aircraft and left. There were no structures close at hand where we could seek shelter from the heat yet still keep an eye on the helicopter. We didn't feel like eating and knew staying with the helicopter would be quite uncomfortable. Oftentimes when we were in situations such as this, where we were shut down and waiting on a mission, we would lie on the floor of the helicopter and try to sleep, or lie beside the aircraft if we were in grass, but this day there would be none of that. With the floor covered in blood and mucus—even if we had a poncho to cover it—I would still not have been able to lie there. To seek refuge beside the aircraft was impossible due to the hot "PSP" (perforated steel planking) landing mats. So, as the sun worked its way westward, we stood and sat alternating seats until the pilots returned around 3:30 p.m. I had hours to think about Kimball and wonder about life and death. I was starting to wear down from the day's events. I was tired and had not wanted to eat. It felt like my body had been in an oven. With the arrival of the pilots, we were advised to return to our base. We cranked up, got our compass heading, and started home.

We were in the air for a while on the way back when we got word our base was under attack. Apparently, the Vietcong were firing rockets or mortars into the installation. We were told to stay away, and they would advise us when it was safe to return. Our pilot decided to fly to a navy installation on the coast to wait it out. I believe it was at Vũng Tàu. As we got closer to the base, the air traffic controller had us make our final approach from the south, taking us over the white sandy beach and beautiful blue water of the South China Sea. We landed, shut the engine down, secured the blades, and headed to the mess hall for supper. I was now hungry, tired, and filthy from the grime and sweat. The meal was delicious, the mess hall air conditioned, and we were even served ice cream for dessert. I was very appreciative but sad to say this was the highlight of the day. We sat there for hours, until, finally, around 11:00 p.m., we got word we could return to our base.

Once again, we cranked up, refueled, and headed home. We decided to slide the cargo doors closed because it can get quite cool at night, especially flying at an altitude of 2000 feet. I don't remember how long the flight was, but, during that time, I stared out the large plexiglass side window. I looked up to see a few stars but there was no moon that night. The only lights I saw were from small fires over the vast delta. Some of the fires were probably small villages but others were from artillery strikes or skirmishes earlier in the day that left soldiers and civilians dead or wounded. I thought about Kimball and the infantry soldiers, my boots resting on their dried blood.

The silence was broken when the pilot keyed the radio and said, "Cowboy 384, Bearcat tower," asking for landing instructions. The voice of the air traffic controller advised us that the base was on emergency power and to use caution due to the limited visibility. We landed and hovered a few feet off the ground until we came to our parking area. Our area, as all the rest, was a wall of sandbags stacked about 5 feet high in the shape of an L. The pilot with the help of the crew chief and gunner would hover sideways until the nose of the ship faced the short end of the L, and the body and tail section was parallel to the long side of the L. This would somewhat protect the helicopter from rockets and mortars. With the engine shut down and blades still slowly turning, the pilots then did a post flight check, while I waited until the blades came to a complete stop before I attempted to secure them. On this night, as I waited, I scanned the flight line for any damage from the attack but saw nothing. The rockets probably landed in another area of the base, but it was so dark, one could have landed 20 feet away and I wouldn't have been able to see the crater. A jeep then came and picked up the pilots, taking them to the operations section so they could complete their log. Jon started his postflight checklist while I secured the ammunition. I only had to remove the linked ammunition belt from each machine gun, neatly fold the ammunition back into its metal container and secure the lids. I laid the machine guns and personal items on top of the sandbags. I then went looking for water to clean the floor.

All of the work that night would have to be accomplished from the beam of our red, six-volt Eveready flashlight. It was almost 1:00 a.m. With a small bucket I walked to the nearest fifty-five-gallon water drum. I shined my light inside, but it was empty. I went to another and found some water, but it wouldn't be enough. I noticed a mud puddle that was fairly large and decided to use the dirty water to scrub the floor and then rinse it with the clean water. It took about thirty minutes for Jon to complete his checklist, and by then I was also finished.

With everything complete, we gathered all our equipment and started walking back to our barracks. As we passed one helicopter after another, I felt such a strange feeling inside of me. I was scared, but I wasn't scared of dying or being captured. I know that sounds silly, but the only way I can explain it is to say I was scared of being lost. And I don't mean being lost and not able to find my way home. This was a different feeling, but at the time I couldn't explain it. I do know I was upset and saddened from all that had happened and felt I wanted to pray. But, up until this time, I had never sincerely prayed to God and didn't know how to. The only words that came to my mind were, "God, I don't think I can fly tomorrow." That prayer was my last thought of the night. As we walked a few more minutes we saw headlights coming our way, and to our surprise, it was our platoon truck coming to pick us up.

We arrived at our company area, and behind the beam of our flashlights we entered our barracks. I followed Jon as we walked the entire length of the hallway until we got to our cubicle, the last one on the left; Kimball's was the last one on the right. Neither of those bunks would be occupied that night. I didn't bother to secure the machine guns in my wall locker due to the fact that I would be getting up in a few hours to fly again, and we were trying to be as quiet as possible. I leaned them against the wall and the locker, slid the barrel bag under my bunk, undressed to my undershorts, and laid on my bed.

The next thing I remember is waking to hot, humid conditions and in the very position I'd laid down. I knew I was the only one in the barracks, as the flight crews had left hours before. As I rolled to a sitting position, I thought of God and of my prayer. I had a strange feeling, but it was more than a feeling, it was something more than that, something deep inside of me that I couldn't explain. I did know I was the "newbie," the newest person in the company, and I discovered I wasn't going to be flying that day. How did this happen, was it orchestrated by God? If anyone was to get a day off, it would be a more senior troop or one who was "short."

Around 8:00 a.m., in the eerie quiet, I slipped on my flip-flops and walked about six paces to the opening of Kimball's cubicle. I stared at his bunk, just the way he'd left it a little over twenty-four hours ago. I did not, or could not, enter the space; next to his bed was an empty wooden ammunition box that had some of his personal effects lying on its top. As I stood there a few minutes, something overcame me. I was sad that Kimball had died, yet there was an overwhelming peace inside of me, a sense of calm. Kimball was dead, and I was alive, so why did I have this calming peace? I now wonder these many years later if my peace was also Kimball's peace.

I cannot remember the rest of my day only that I spent a short time in the enlisted men's club where I drank a Coke and listened to "Everybody's Talkin'," a popular song at the time. When the flight crews returned that evening there was still sadness in the air. Not one person said anything about me not flying. It was as if I had flown, and we were all returning from an uneventful flight. The platoon sergeant came and gathered Kimball's belongings. A few days later a new gunner was assigned to the company and moved his belongings into Kimball's area.

The next morning the platoon was awakened, and the routine started again, except I was a different young man. A seed was planted, a seed of faith in something spiritual that was going to redirect my life. I've pondered that last day in March, now so long ago. My heart has changed, my sadness grown for those killed that day and those who survived yet still struggle with the emotional consequences of an unjust war. I think of Kimball. I touch his name on panel 12W, line 63, at the Vietnam Memorial. I sometimes wonder if me not flying that next day was due to Jon going to our platoon sergeant to express his concern for me. Maybe he saw the pain in my face and Jon, having a kind compassionate heart, reached out to the sergeant. Whether Jon intervened or God intervened I'll never know, but I do know something spiritual was developing in my inner soul.

. . .

A week or so had passed since Kimball's death and we happened to be flying a single-ship mission. One of our pilots mentioned visiting the remaining crew member who was still in the hospital. Of the three crew members, the pilots had sustained minor wounds. The copilot returned to active duty. The pilot, because his time in Vietnam was coming to an end, returned to the States. I cannot remember the location or the name of the hospital we flew to. We landed and parked our helicopter in the same area as the "DUSTOFF" helicopters. DUSTOFF was a call sign for the medical evacuation helicopters, flying ambulances with white crosses painted on the nose and each side cargo door. We entered through the main doors from the helipad into the triage area of the hospital. They weren't busy at this time but by the sight of things they had been. The pilots seemed to know where to go, so Jon and I followed.

Off of a main corridor we entered the burn ward. There was bed after bed of soldiers recovering from burns. The door gunner was about two-thirds of the way down on the left side of the room. The first thing that hit me was the smell of the ointment used on the burns. I don't believe it's used today, and I'm certain we wouldn't be able to enter just dressed in our flight suits. The door gunner was lying on his stomach with a white sheet made into a tent so as not to touch his second and third degree burns on his backside and lower back. It looked horrible, and I started to feel squeamish, thinking I may faint. I excused myself and made it to the hallway without fainting or throwing up. I leaned up against the ward wall, lowered myself to a squat, and placed my head between my knees. I immediately felt better. The gunner would recover but most likely have terrible scars when he finally healed.

· · ·

Jon Dixon and I shared the same small cubicle, his bunk against one wall, mine against the other. We each had a footlocker and a small metal wall locker. Jon had a love for Formula One racing cars and hoped to be a professional driver one day. His girlfriend sent him racing magazines. She would read them cover to cover, underline important information, and add notes; she loved him dearly. He never became a Formula One race car driver but did earn a PhD and now teaches aerospace engineering at a university. Jon was definitely smart, dedicated, and took his crew-chief responsibilities seriously. I remember every so many hours the "short shaft," which connected the transmission to the main rotor blade assembly, had to be removed and maintained. It was the crew chief's job to perform this maintenance along with other important duties. Jon was very methodical and did everything with care and neatness. Even when he safety wired a bolt or fitting it was always done perfectly—the wire wraps were smooth and uniform. I was very fortunate to be assigned to Jon.

If we had access to a portable water tank trailer, Jon would take the opportunity to give 384 a bath. I enjoyed this. I would open the top hatch and lower myself down into the cool water. I'd rest my arms on the round lip of the tank and watch the overflow escape over the rim and down the sides. These trailers didn't have pumps, so we had to use buckets to apply the water. Jon would climb on top of the helicopter, and I would pass a bucket of water to him. He then would wet a section of the ship, and scrub with soapy water using a long handle scrub brush. My job was to supply clean rinse water to Jon before the soapy water dried. We weren't too concerned about how wet we got. It was cooling to our shirtless skin, and I considered it quite fun.

. . .

One thing that has bothered me since my tour of duty is my part in taking lives in an unnecessary war. I first justified it as being part of war, but now I no longer justify it at all. The first person I helped kill was fairly early in my tour: One lone Vietcong soldier decided to make a dash across an open rice paddy. I didn't see this person until the copilot said over the radio "got one running." It took me less than a second to see this person frantically running shin deep in muddy brown water. As I slid farther out to the edge of my canvas seat and pointed the machine gun, I could see out of my peripheral vision another helicopter also bearing down on this one person. This solitary soldier was now running in front of and between two helicopters. The gross enormity of noise, machines, and arms against one human being is so clear to me now. I knew in an instant there would be no escape for this young person. When our bullets struck the muddy water it sent up narrow sprays 3 feet high. In the middle of it, the body just dropped into the brown paddy water. No flip, no summersault, no outstretched arms—just a collapse, like a doll filled with sand. We just kept flying on, but I looked back and saw someone who had been alive barely seconds ago cease to exist. Now it was just a body left face down in the muddy water. I don't know for sure if this person was a young man or a young woman, as so many women fought and were killed without discretion. I never forgot that young life: Were they married?Did they keep pictures wrapped in plastic and tucked in a pocket or pack? The life that was ended that day has remained in my mind ever since and has had a deep effect on who I've become. In that respect, perhaps, the life of that soldier continued on by affecting the humanity of another.

. . .

One morning around 9 o'clock, Jon and I were walking back to our barracks from the flight line. We weren't flying that day because 384 was in for maintenance, but there were some duties in and around the helicopter Jon was required to do. He always chose to perform these duties early in the morning before it got too hot. I would accompany Jon to assist him any way I could. Our walk took us down a long stretch of dusty road that ran parallel to the concertina wire on the north side of the base. On the shoulder of this road, grass had grown quite high and needed to be mowed or cut down.

The army hired Vietnamese women to perform this task using sickles to cut the grass at ground level. As we made our way down the road, we came upon eight to ten Vietnamese women working. Even though it was only 9:00 a.m., it was quite hot and humid and there was no shade. They were wearing their traditional dress of black silk-like pajama pants and shirts, sandal shoes and straw hats. As we walked by, I looked at them working and felt sorry that they had to do such labor-intensive work in such conditions. But what stands out in my mind was their lunch. About 20 feet away from where they were working, lying side by side in the cut grass was ten small, clear plastic bags with a mixture of rice and fish sauce. They were just sitting there, no protection from the bugs or sun. I was saddened to see people having to work and survive in such conditions. Then to survey the road, to see how much work they had ahead of them, it was disheartening to me and I'm sure for them as well. I think about those women and wonder what life was like after we left, and when the North Vietnamese took over the entire country.

. . .

One early afternoon we were ordered to pick up some captured enemy soldiers. The pick up zone was an easy place to land. We've encountered some pick up and landing zones that were quite tight and somewhat difficult, but most of the pilots I flew with were quite good with many flight hours under their belt. I was impressed more than once with their flying abilities. When it came to tough situations, especially when called in to pick up wounded, they were outstanding and courageous. As we descended that afternoon, I could see three prisoners tightly secured with rope. We landed on dry grass that was about 8 inches high, whipping it back and forth from the rotor wash. These prisoners didn't have their eyes covered as some we'd transported. We sat them on the dirty aluminum floor along with one infantry soldier assigned to guard them. They didn't appear to be wounded, but by the appearance of their tattered uniforms they'd seen combat up close and personal. They sat quietly, and though I didn't see any fear in their faces, they did look tired and worn out, yet calm. They were lean and hardened, most likely from months or maybe even years of fighting and living in harsh conditions. They too were brothers in arms fighting for a cause they believed in. As we flew to our destination, there was something about these soldiers that must have impacted me. Why would this incident stir my heart all these years later? I believe they were probably my same age, but they appeared older, more mature. I didn't have a dislike or hatred towards them. I respected them, even felt compassion toward them because they too were also brothers in arms.

I don't remember the facility we transported them to and don't know their fate. I'm sad to write that these veterans were most likely tortured to obtain information, then imprisoned or executed. The horror, brutality, and insanity of war . . .

One other casualty of the Vietnam War was the deaths of servicemen due to drug overdose. At that time, I didn't drink alcohol and was quite ignorant of drugs. I knew soldiers who drank but none who took drugs.

I had heard if you wanted some good drugs to visit "the Thais on the berm." The Thais were soldiers from Thailand who were assigned to guard our base perimeter, and the berm was a built-up mound of sandbags or dirt for protection. I had no interest in visiting them but apparently some US soldiers did.

I do remember one helicopter maintenance worker who overdosed and died, apparently due to drugs combined with alcohol. I don't remember his name, but I do remember him as having a likable demeanor, with a strong athletic build. When he was assigned to work on our helicopter, he was always enthusiastic and appeared to be quite knowledgeable. I was usually in the background; most conversations were between him and Jon. At that time, I didn't know a great deal about helicopter repairs, but I knew the importance of having a knowledgeable competent repairman doing such tasks. I was sad when I found out he had died. His death, as many others, was listed as a noncombat casualty of this war. His name is also etched on the Vietnam Memorial.

· · ·

Not all of our missions were combat. At times we were given an assignment to be a taxi service. We would fly, as we had many times, in that same single-ship mission, to transport personnel and materials to different destinations. We might fly mail, food rations, or ammunition to an infantry platoon or a rock and roll band from the States or other countries to perform for the troops. Usually, all locations we were to fly to were considered secure, so we weren't overly concerned about manning the machine guns.

One such mission was to deliver a manila packet to an orphanage run by French Catholic nuns. Apparently, they knew about what time we were to arrive or possibly heard our helicopter's distinct sound approaching, but the nuns had taken the time to line up twenty or so children in perfect order of height in front of the orphanage.

We landed in short lush green grass about 150 feet from the clay and brick structure, washing the children with cool air from our rotor blades. They all had a big smile and waved but never broke their position in line. One of the nuns in her long black-and-white habit walked up to the pilot's door, and he handed her the packet. After the nun returned to the children, we lifted off and I waved goodbye. We crossed over a tree line and were soon over a dense jungle. I was still thinking of the nuns and children when there was a muffled small arms gunfire. Luckily, no one was hit, nor was the helicopter. It happened so quickly we didn't have time to react. I don't remember if the pilots even reported the incident. We didn't investigate but just flew on. This war in Vietnam, and, I guess, all wars, was so unpredictable. One minute we were interacting with an orphanage and then just a few miles from their location we encountered the enemy. As for the nuns and the children of the orphanage I've often wondered what became of them. As I write this, my granddaughter, Autumn, is nine, the same age as some of these orphans. As I ponder my love for Autumn, I vividly see those little ones so perfectly in line, and I feel that same love for them.

. . .

Six days after we invaded Cambodia, the Army National Guard shot and killed four students, and wounded nine others, at Kent State University. For some soldiers, these two events—the invasion of Cambodia and the events at Kent State—would be deciding factors that shaped their opinion about the war. One day, I was assigned to fly with another crew chief on his aircraft. He was a seasoned veteran who was returning to the States not long after. He kept up with current affairs and was angry with what happened at Kent State. He told the crew members that when he returned home that he was going to protest the war. At the time, I wasn't mature or knowledgeable enough to understand the politics of the war, but, in time, I would come to my own conclusion about the war and its effect.

. . .

Early one morning as Jon and I readied the helicopter for flight, we were told to install two canvas jump seats because we were to fly to Red Carpet, Long Bien, to transport six personnel to different locations. Helicopter 384 did have a canvas bench seat that folded up against the back wall of the aircraft, separating the engine and transmission from the crew compartment. This seat could hold four personnel. But since we were told six people would be transported, we needed two more seats. Though they could have sat on the floor like the infantry soldiers, we wanted to offer better accommodations. These two seats sat back-to-back just behind the pilots' seats. When secured they faced sideways, looking out the side of the helicopter. Two of the six were "Donut Dollies," young ladies who volunteered for the Red Cross. In doing some research, I learned about a Red Cross program called Supplemental Recreational Activities Overseas (SRAO), which hosted these volunteers. To qualify they had to have a college degree and commit to a year in Vietnam. The Red Cross organization didn't like the use of the name Donut Dollies, as they felt it was too demeaning, but the name stuck. And I believe today the term is well respected by both military personnel and the ladies who participated in this admirable yet dangerous cause.

Red Carpet I think got its name from the fact that VIPs would be flown to its fairly large command center. Even though Red Carpet was a fancy name for a helicopter pad, it wasn't all that large. Landing wasn't too difficult but taking off could be a problem because of how small it was, especially with a heavy load on a hot humid day. Oftentimes, in the middle of the day when it was very hot and humid, some helicopters, especially loaded to maximum capacity, had to take off somewhat like a fixed-wing aircraft. They needed a little runway to get some momentum to help with the lift.

Jon would decide where everyone would sit. Two soldiers would ride in each well of the aircraft, where Jon and I usually sat for inserting troops to man the machine guns. The Donut Dollies were kept together and placed on the canvas bench seat, and the remaining soldiers would occupy the two jump seats. Jon felt this was good weight distribution. We would sit next to the Donut Dollies, so we could operate the sliding doors. With all personnel in their designated seat, we hovered a few feet off the ground to the middle of the short runway. When the pilot had 384's nose facing down the runway, he had Jon and myself assist him in backing up as far as he could, so he'd have as much runway as possible to take off.

Jon and I had decided before takeoff that we would close the sliding door on each side of the aircraft. Our decision was based on the cool air and wind turbulence waiting for us at 2000 feet. The doors would have to stay open until we started to lift off. Then we would slide the doors closed at the same time. I was told if one door was closed well before the other, it could make handling somewhat difficult. The pilots would always check with Jon and me before they took off to make sure both sides and rear of the aircraft were clear. With the doors still open, Jon and I were able to lean out to respond to the pilot's request for clearance. If everything was okay, Jon would key his microphone and say, "Clear left," and I would repeat with "Clear right."

With the aircraft backed as far as possible the pilot proceeded forward. As he gained speed, he then nosed the aircraft forward or slightly down, our signal to slide the doors closed. Just as the doors made contact with the latches, I heard a bang. With a blink of an eye the helicopter pivoted ninety degrees to the left. I looked over at Jon thinking we did something to cause this problem, but it took only a split second to know we were going to crash. I looked forward and saw the pilot making quick adjustments with the controls. When we slammed into the ground the skid on my side collapsed and bent the door. One of the rotor blades somehow sliced the tail section in two and threw it to the side. With the momentum of the helicopter still moving forward, the aircraft started to slide, heading for a row of bunkers. For a brief second, I thought we were going to roll over, entrapping us and more likely causing serious injuries. Luckily, we didn't, and we finally came to a stop. Jon was able to get his door open with no problem and grab the fire extinguisher. He then went to assist the pilots out of their seats. I climbed over the passengers who were thrown about in order to open my door. I could only slide it about 8 or 10 inches but was able to wedge my slim frame halfway through the opening, bracing my back against the bulkhead next to and behind the pilot's seat. Pushing with all my strength I was able to slide the door open enough to get people out. The first person out the door was one of the Red Cross workers. I told her to run to a bunker that was parallel to the runway. I didn't realize until she started running that the helicopter was leaning downward at a fairly steep angle. With the engine winding down, I noticed the remaining rotor blade making its downward sweep. I turned and yelled to the young lady "duck!" I don't know if she heard me at that distance over the noise of the damaged engine, but she must have sensed or saw something, because she did duck her head and the tip of the blade hit the top of her beehive hairdo. If she hadn't lowered her head, the blade would have surely killed her. After that incident, all others were directed forward of the aircraft to safety. There were no major injuries, just cuts and bruises. The cause of the crash was due to engine failure. Apparently, a blade from one of the turbine wheels had broken free, causing the engine to fail. These blades were fairly small but just one coming unattached caused the crash of this once strong and reliable helicopter and almost the death of its occupants.

A crane truck arrived along with a lowboy trailer pulled by a massive military tractor. The crane then loaded the fuselage and tail section onto the trailer. Cowboy 384 was then hauled to a helicopter graveyard where it would be used for parts. I don't remember where our old friend was taken, but Jon and I rode on the trailer next to 384 to the "cemetery." We were like honored pall bearers, its closest family members.

We did manage to retrieve the tail rotor chain. This stainless-steel chain was precision made and was responsible for delivering power to the tail rotor. The chain ran from a gearbox at the very end of the tail section up to another gearbox to turn the tail rotor. I believe it was Jon who told me it was a tradition to wear an arm bracelet made from this chain to show you had survived a helicopter crash. Jon gave me a section and since I had the addresses of the two Red Cross ladies who sent us photos they had taken of the crash, I made two bracelets for them. I hope they received them; I believe those chains may have gained meaning and importance these many years later. Now with the loss of 384, Jon and I would have to be content with flying other helicopters that weren't her caliber. Luckily for Jon, he was getting short, and I was glad he didn't have to endure that for too long since he was with 384 for such a longer time.

. . .

I can only remember one occasion getting into a fight. It was in the sixth grade and confronted a fellow classmate who was somewhat of a bully. Our confrontation lasted only a few seconds when he responded with a well-placed punch to my neck just below my chin. The fight was over; I was down gasping for breath.

The other time I physically fought someone, again lasting only a few seconds, was during my tour in Vietnam, and my opponent was a South Vietnam army soldier. We had just finished inserting the first lift of soldiers into a landing zone and had returned for the second and last lift. As the ten soldiers began loading, they observed the hundreds of empty machine gun cartridge casings that littered the floor plus the off-white color of the machine gun barrels. They were most likely unaware the landing zone wasn't hot. We encountered no enemy and did not receive any small arms fire. With all troops loaded, we took off and headed for the landing zone. After clearing a western tree line, we dropped rapidly into an open rice paddy. Again, we received no incoming fire but did use our machine guns to shoot into the tree lines, making sure we fired over the heads of the previous insertion of soldiers who were staying behind the rice paddy dikes.

We abruptly came to a hover a foot or two off the brown paddy water, and the troops, as usual, were anxious to get off and find cover, so I was somewhat surprised to see one soldier waiting at the open doorway acting strange. As I provided cover fire, I signaled for him to get off; by this time, the pilot had noticed the situation and told me to get him off. I immediately placed my gun on the floor and within seconds we were in a wrestling match. The last thing I heard before my communications link was disconnected from my flight helmet was "throw him off." I didn't know why he didn't want to get off, but I followed orders. He may have just been scared. Jon, in his haste to help me, became entangled in his belt of linked M60 ammunition. One advantage I had over this soldier was my size; though I was only 165 pounds I outweighed him by probably 20 pounds. Since I had on a flight helmet I wasn't concerned about any blows to my head. As we thrashed around, the pilot had difficulty keeping the helicopter stable, we started to swing side to side, so the pilot had to add lift to prevent the blades from striking the water. With us gaining altitude and swaying side to side he was concerned we both may fall out. I was able to pin him face down to the floor, and with that I picked him up around the waist and flung him overboard. As I released him, I noticed we were now about 15 feet off the ground; luckily, he landed feet first, driving him knee deep in the muddy brown water of the paddy.

I could see the pilots signaling to me that we needed to get out of there. Seeing the soldier's M16 rifle still on the floor, I removed the magazine of ammunition and threw it to him, landing a few feet out of his reach. With his legs suctioned to the soft bottom of the paddy he did his best to lunge for the rifle. The last thing I saw was him bringing the rifle to his shoulder as to fire, but we banked hard left so he couldn't get a shot at me or the pilot in the right seat. I knew as soon as I let the rifle fly that I didn't take the time to check if there was a round chambered, therefore giving him one shot. We never knew what became of that soldier; we were just grateful to be out of that situation.

. . .

I was never wounded but came close a few times. To experience bullets whizzing by and none hitting you or to feel the displacement of air and then the explosive sound of a rocket attack was interesting to say the least. The hot sting of spent cartridges lodged between my backside and the canvas seat is now only a memory. I will never forget the smell of smoke canisters, burnt grass, and spent cartridges.

One other smell that was quite disgustingly pungent was the outdoor urinals. One such urinal, that just happened to be placed near the shower facility, was a fifty-five-gallon metal drum buried up to the top. Across the top was metal window screen haphazardly secured over it. It likely had holes cut in the bottom for drainage, but I had no way of knowing. It didn't matter anyway because it was always full to the top, even to the point of spilling over. Luckily, we had built a wooden boardwalk and a platform to stand on so as not to have our feet come in contact with the putrid liquid.

One hot afternoon when I wasn't flying for one reason or another, I decided to take a nap after lunch. I laid down on my back on top of my nylon camouflaged poncho liner. I knew it would be hot and humid, but I was just so tired. It didn't take long before I fell into a deep sleep that lasted for a good couple of hours. When I woke, I felt groggy and needed to pee. I stepped out the back screen door of the barracks and walked the wooden boardwalk to the urinal. Even as groggy as I was, I knew to take a deep breath, and hold it, just prior to arriving so as not to breathe the foul smell.

I'm standing there urinating, still half asleep when a round from a 105 mm howitzer was fired about 50 yards away. It definitely woke me up. My stream came to an abrupt halt and my heart felt like it was going to jump from my chest. This 105 mm howitzer was one of three artillery guns positioned inside a circle of stacked sandbags at the perimeter of our base camp. It wasn't uncommon to hear a round fired at random times throughout the day. They were called harassment rounds, fired at a location they felt the enemy may be occupying. I now wonder all these years later if some of those rounds exploded by a farmer or their water buffalo plowing the field. Some of those rounds never did explode upon impact, waiting for years to be uncovered by children playing or a farmer plowing their paddies or fields. Another sad consequence of war is this kind of delayed toll on innocent civilians that, in some cases, could have been avoided.

There was a difference between the sound of artillery depending on if it was outgoing or incoming. Outgoing, as experienced from the urinal story, only makes one loud ear-piercing explosive noise. Incoming artillery has two dimensions. The first dimension is from the round as it detonates and a shock wave is sent out. It felt to me like the displacement of air. Within a split second came the explosive sound. The explosive power of these projectiles was truly frightening.

One late night I was sound asleep in my bunk and was woken by the sound of explosions. At first, they were quite far off but became louder and louder as the enemy fired rockets into our compound. The Vietcong were "walking them in." They would fire one rocket or mortar and then make a slight calibration on their tubes, a calibration that would send the next projectile deeper into the compound. They continued this tactic until they expended their ammunition or were run off.

It wasn't long until we knew we needed to get to the bunker across from the front door of our barracks. We never liked going into the bunker. Because it was below ground, it usually had standing water in it and was a home for rats. But with these rounds landing closer and closer the bunker was a welcome fortified structure. I pulled up my mosquito net, threw off my poncho liner, and sat up. After taking the time to put on my flip-flops, I headed out the door in my olive drab, army-issued boxer shorts. As I contemplated the large puddle of water between me and the bunker, a rocket exploded behind our barracks, and the blast of air displacement hit me. I went flying sideways. I lost one flip-flop but made it into the bunker to huddle down with other soldiers. I wasn't hit by shrapnel, but I must have come close. Although this was scary, that was the last rocket fired and then it was over. The enemy used this tactic fairly often, firing a few rockets or mortars then melting away.

That was one of only two times that I experienced incoming rounds. Fortunately for us, I don't think, at least at that time, that the Vietcong, nor the North Vietnamese Army, had heavy artillery pieces in our area. I can't imagine what it must be like to experience a salvo of incoming rounds from heavy artillery pieces, like my Uncle Bill endured from the German Army in the Arden Forest. I felt so small and insignificant in the face of the destructive power and force of even the smaller rockets and mortars, yet I was somewhat protected in our fortified sandbagged bunker. But to be caught out in the open, under a heavy artillery strike without even a shallow hole to curl up in had to be over-the-top frightening.

Helicopters or any aircraft flying in a war zone had to be aware of artillery fire. To fly into or through an artillery strike is certainly dangerous. The pilots did their best to obtain any information on artillery being fired, including its direction and targets. Numerous helicopters have been downed by friendly fire from artillery.

One other concern was helicopters coming in contact with another helicopter in flight. The pilots and crew members were always keeping an eye out. But we did come very close to a midair collision one night. Usually, we didn't insert ground troops at night, but tonight was going to be an exception. This nighttime insertion mission was a first for our entire crew, though I didn't hear any grumbling or discussion. We did as we were ordered and prepared the helicopter. As I remember, our day missions were uneventful but still long and stressful, which added to mental tiredness that night.

I somewhat remember it between 5:00 and 6:00 p.m. Our company commander, who would command the flight, and his driver stopped at each helicopter. The commander got out of his jeep and personally handed each of us a box of C rations and a fairly cold Coca-Cola. I wasn't hungry but the Coke was very appreciative.

C rations were a meal in a small, brown, thin cardboard box about 3 to 4 inches wide, 5 to 6 inches long, and about the same deep. The ones we had were called "B-2 units" and contained a small can of beanie weenies (my favorite), spaghetti with meatballs, or, maybe, ham and lima beans. These were the ones I remember but there were more varieties. I also remember that the crackers, pound cake, and peaches were all well received. There was also a chocolate bar, cigarettes, salt and pepper, toilet paper, a plastic spoon, and a can-opener called a "P38."

We took off as a flight of five helicopters, and I don't recall any gunship helicopters going with us. We flew a fairly short distance to our pickup landing zone somewhere close to Vinh Long. The infantry soldiers were in their usual small huddles of eight to ten soldiers, each group separated by a distance that allowed the helicopters to land one behind the other. In this way, each group could board the helicopter in front of them making for an orderly and quick boarding. The backbone of the military knew exactly how to board and where to sit. Some soldiers rested their backs against the pilots' seat and next to the console between their seats. Some sat cross-legged in the middle of the dimpled aluminum floor. A couple rested their back against the padded bulkhead wall that separated the transmission from the cargo area. And some sat on the edge with their lower legs dangling outside the helicopter. I always had respect and compassion for these soldiers; they had the most dangerous assignments and the filthiest living conditions, yet they risked their lives for a cause they may or may not have believed in.

With all soldiers loaded and ready, the flight was ordered to depart. The lead helicopter would be the first to take off, then the second would follow close behind with the third close behind them, and so on, until all aircraft were airborne. Ours was the third helicopter in the flight, and as we gained altitude, the string of helicopters moved to their right so we were flying in a modified V formation. If you've seen geese flying in formation, you get the picture. This is a fairly safe formation for numerous aircraft to fly in. Everyone knows their position and keys off the helicopter to their left. But since it was a nighttime mission, we couldn't see very well beyond the helicopters on either side of us. We could really only see clearance lights, so we had to be much more cautious. One other concern was small arms fire. Those small clearance lights could possibly give the enemy a good target. But if they did fire on us, we could possibly see their tracer rounds exposing their position.

All seemed fine. The marker lights on the helicopter next to us seemed an appropriately safe distance away. Then, out of nowhere, a helicopter zoomed between us. It sliced its way from behind us at a slightly lower altitude between us and the helicopter to our right and, in a flash, darted out in front of us while it rose in altitude. It happened so fast that I could only key my intercom radio and say "wow." The right seat pilot said over the radio, "Where did he come from?" and the pilot on the helicopter to our right used profanity to express his surprise. They were so close, I could see the faces of the soldiers dangling their legs over the side. I believe our blades may have overlapped or, in the least, came very close. Luckily it happened so very quickly, and no contact was made. If it had, I would not be writing this now.

I don't remember much else about the rest of the mission. We came so close to disaster yet there wasn't another word mentioned.

. . .

Early one morning we were assigned to fly a single-ship mission. I was somewhat relieved; we wouldn't be inserting troops that day (but I reminded myself that could always change). For some reason I was unusually tired, not so much physically but mentally. It was overcast with no rain predicted. It was just dreary, which didn't help with my funk or well-being. Everything was gray or olive drab, the helicopters, the sandbags, the dusty buildings, the countryside, the sky. With the pilots secured into their seats I untied the nylon strap attached to the rod that secured the rotor blades to the tail section.

After I informed the pilots they were clear, they proceeded to start the turbine jet engine. The starting of this engine makes a different sound than starting an automobile—to me it always sounded like a cross between a hum and a whine—and with that the rotor blades began to turn ever so slowly. As the sound increased in pitch the blade revolutions stayed in sync as they were supposed to. Next, I donned my flight helmet. I would need to communicate with the pilots and Jon. I jumped aboard and sat at my end of the fold-down canvas bench seat. Jon was already aboard sitting at his end. It would take about three minutes or so for all systems to come to their correct temperature and pressures. I sat there in a relaxed state feeling the helicopter's vibrations moving through my body. As the vibrations increased in tempo, jerking the helicopter in every direction, there was a brief period where the vibration changes somewhat, and became rhythmic, even soothing. This would be fleeting, however, as power increased.

Once at full power, the copilot asked if we were clear. Jon leaned out his open door and scanned the area and tail section on his side. "Clear, left," he said, and I, in turn, checked, and said, "Clear right." I looked down at the skid on my side, where it seemed to lose its support of the aircraft, maybe slightly relaxing as we separated from the ground.

We taxied sideways to our left out of our L-shaped revetment of sand-bags. Clear of obstacles, the pilot rotated us 90 degrees to his left. We were now facing in the westwardly direction. We continued to hover forward a few feet off the ground until we reached the taxi way. The copilot then contacted air traffic control for takeoff instructions. Not only were there numerous helicopters at our base but also fixed wing aircraft, so caution was always in order. We received our takeoff instructions as we crept up to the main runway. Given clearances for takeoff, the copilot now rotated 90 degrees to his right and proceeded down the outside edge of the main runway. Gaining speed and adding height he gracefully nosed the aircraft ever so slightly downward, and we worked our way skyward. Our turbulence with the ground soon dissipated as we continued climbing. We were heading north. To our east was the South China Sea and Cambodia to the west.

Clearing the outer perimeter of the concertina wire we continued to climb, I felt heavy on my seat. We started through the dense, dark cloud cover and soon after popped right out. Now we were flying about 10 feet above a beautiful flat blanket of thick white clouds that stretched as far as I could see. To my right the sun was shining, and the sky was a magnificent deep blue. This had my attention. What was moments before dark and gray was now white and crisp. Here we were all alone skimming over a blanket of clouds I felt I could walk on. The brutality of war and death below us seemed far away. Though it was short-lived, the aircraft commander felt we should gain more altitude fearing other aircraft could pop up out of the clouds causing a collision. I understood his concern, but the additional altitude took away from the serenity, and my peacefulness was gone. Though the experience was brief, this scene was photographed by my mind and has always been with me.

. . .

Sometimes the smallest things will stay with us for a lifetime. I wasn't a coffee drinker at nineteen, but for some reason I felt like having a cup. As a boy, my father took me fishing or duck hunting and always brought a thermos of coffee leaving just enough room at the top to add some milk and sugar. Usually around 9:00 a.m. he would pour us a cup and have a few Hydrox cookies with it. Dad always gave me the red plastic cup that served as the thermos lid. I remember it had a little handle, but I didn't need it because by midmorning the coffee was just the right temperature. I've never tasted coffee that good. Dad always dunked his cookies in his coffee, but I never did. What wonderful memories.

It was fairly late in the evening, around 10:00 p.m. Our barracks happened to be one of the farthest from the mess hall. The distance between them wasn't a big deal, but the heavy rain that night could have been. However I was set on having a cup of coffee. I donned my rain jacket and "Boonie" hat and headed out towards the mess hall. The mess hall was always open. In fact, if we came in late from a flight, they always made us something to eat. I appreciated the cooks; they had a thankless unglamorous job. I was once in the mess hall late one evening when a helicopter maintenance worker came in on his break. He started making fun of a new cook serving scrambled eggs. He called out to some of his buddies, "We got a new spoon." Spoon was the word used to disrespect the cooks. I felt bad for the new guy and angry towards the maintenance worker.

As I made my way to the mess hall, I was able to stay on the wooden boardwalk pretty much the entire trip, so my boots didn't get soaked through. I entered the warm mess hall, taking off my raincoat and hat and hanging them up to drip on the concrete floor. There were only a few people in the dining area. I served myself and added some milk, just like my father did. I picked out a table and sat down. I didn't know the few troops in the dining room and didn't know the night shift cooks but I enjoyed the warmth of the setting as it poured outside. It was comforting, and I even enjoyed the coffee I hardly ever drank. I don't remember how long I stayed or the walk back to my barracks, and I don't recall having any problems falling to sleep. All these years later I'm comforted by these types of memories. I've found the memories and experiences that might be considered the least important in a worldly sense have had the most impact on my heart.

I did learn one important lesson from a lunch at this same mess hall. I'd selected milk to drink with my meal. In Vietnam, milk came, if I remember correctly, in quart paper cartons. They were kept in a large aluminum steel pan covered in a thin layer of ice. During basic training, it was kept in cold dispensers. You held your cup under the spout, lifted the heavy chrome handle, and the cold fresh milk flowed into the cup. I open the container by folding the two sides open and back, then squeezed the sides to open the spout. Since I was quite thirsty, I immediately took a large couple of swallows. As I went to set the milk back on the table, I discovered it was spoiled. I think I had downed about a third of the container. I didn't get sick, but it made me wince. From that point forward I always smell milk before I pour.

. . .

I had been told that the job of a helicopter door gunner was one of the most dangerous jobs in combat, but I disagree. It was dangerous, as is any job in a war zone, but in my mind the infantry soldiers, or grunts as they were called, had the most dangerous job by far. We had a good rapport, because they knew we would risk life and helicopter to extract their wounded, and, in turn, they would fiercely cover our landing and take-off to the best of their ability. My heart always went out to those troops when we entered a hot landing zone. We'd come in fast, laying down cover fire with our machine guns, and at the last second hover a foot or two off the ground while the troops scrambled to get off and secure immediate cover.

They had it miserable in the heat and humidity, with the leaches and biting bugs of the Mekong River Delta, and with the constant threat of being killed by enemy forces.

One late afternoon we were heading back to our base after a long grimy day of inserting troops when we were singled out from the flight. We were flying in the "trail" position, the last helicopter in the flight. It was common to redirect the last helicopter if it was needed for another mission. We were told we were needed to resupply a platoon with ammunition and rations. We banked to the right out of the formation and headed to the designated facility where we secured M16 and M60 ammunition and C rations. As we made our way to the platoon's location, the skies were threatening rain, being it was the start of the monsoon season. With the darkish heavy cloud cover, I sensed danger, and pitied the grunts having to be out there all night. The pilot said, "I believe they should be just ahead over the next tree line." As we skimmed over the tree line, there they were, set up in a circle at the edge of an open field with grass about 2 feet high. A red smoke canister was activated, and we were directed to land just east of the smoke, we were also advised to be aware of the wire. The wire was grunt lingo for the trip wire attached to their claymore mines. We could see it from the air quite easily, this wire snaking its way through the grass. We landed, and six soldiers moved quickly to retrieve their needed supplies from us. As I helped them by sliding the boxes across the dirty aluminum floor, I could see up close how filthy and ragged they were. Their fatigues were worn and torn, faces dirty, and their hands and fingernails were encrusted with grime from days or even weeks of not bathing. I felt sorry for them, with the smell of rain in the air they would certainly get no rest tonight.

I do know that sometimes they would set up like they did in this area but after dark would quietly move to another location to possibly lure the enemy to attack this old location thus giving them the opportunity to ambush them. As we lifted off and I looked back at their defenses, I was so thankful I wasn't in their boots. We would arrive back at our base camp in about fifteen or twenty minutes. After postflight and duties, we could get a decent hot meal, maybe take a shower if there was any shower water, and get a somewhat good night's rest. But not for the grunts; they would not have that luxury.

One evening after a hot grimy day of flying, I'd hoped there was water for a shower. Our shower facility was a large steel water tank mounted on top of wooden timbers. The floor beneath was a poured concrete slab. The wooden walls extended maybe 6 feet high with screen material another couple of feet above that. It had a ceiling, but I don't remember if it was wood or metal. I don't remember any lighting inside the shower room, but there was enough light, and this was maybe due to the lighting from the compound. The entrance was a single screen door. At the bottom of the tank a single galvanized pipe extended down through the ceiling where it branched off to numerous open-ended pipes with screw turn valves just above the opening to control the flow of water. If the tank was filled early in the day and no cloud cover, the hot sun would heat the water tank turning the cold water into a nice warm shower. If the tank was filled late in the afternoon or on a rainy day, the water would not warm up making for a quite cold shower. It may have been unpleasant and cold but still appreciated. The bummer was no water at all, making for a grimy and sticky night's sleep.

This particular evening, I slipped on my flip-flops, grabbed my towel and flashlight, and started my trip down the boardwalk. As I proceeded, I used my flashlight to guide my way. I could see the rats between the boards on the boardwalk being herded in front of me. When I got to the shower they scurried out the open end in every direction. Rats were a common sight around the company area. In fact, it was very important to secure or tuck your mosquito net under your mattress when you went to bed—you weren't just keeping out mosquitoes but also rats and mice.

After arriving at the shower, the first thing I did was check for water. If it flowed with a fair amount of velocity, I was quite certain I could finish my shower without running out of water. Tonight, I was fortunate. There was warm water with a good velocity, and I was appreciative. A few minutes later another door gunner entered, a member of the gunship platoon, known as the Falcons. The Falcons provided cover for the flight of helicopters that inserted the ground troops. They flew "lower level," often referred to as "treetop level," and were armed with rockets and machine guns. They also flew slower, as in knots or speed, and staying closer to the ground made them an easier target for small arms fire. As we showered, this Falcons gunner made mention of a small narrow crease on the outside of his left thigh. Apparently a bullet caused the wound, he said, but he wasn't going to report it. He had been wounded twice before, so if he reported it, they would give him a third Purple Heart and he'd have to leave Vietnam. According to him, army regulations stated that if receiving three Purple Hearts on one tour of duty, meant an automatic reassignment—either back to the States or to another part of the world. He made it perfectly clear he didn't want to leave Vietnam. He shared that he had a dislike for the Vietnamese people that verged on hate. He talked about how he liked to kill them . . . enemy, civilian, didn't matter to him. He talked about taking potshots at peasant farmers and their water buffaloes. I hadn't been in Vietnam as long as this young man and was somewhat intimidated by him. I felt being a gunship door gunner held a higher status than a troop-carrying gunner. I did wonder how he was able to keep this third wound quiet. It certainly looked like a bullet nicked his leg. I even thought it may need a few stitches. At the time I didn't doubt his dislike for the Vietnamese people and hoped his talk about taking potshots at civilians was only talk. What became of this young man? If he's alive, does he still hold that hatred? Has it destroyed him? I'd like to hope he's had a change of heart and mind, as time, age, and life experiences can do that.

As for me, all these years later, I've certainly had a change of heart. The person I've become, my thoughts, my feelings were directly influenced by my time spent in military service. As much as war is truly terrible, it can have a way of impacting lives in a good or positive way, but it can also bring destruction to the minds of some individuals. I think I was fortunate to have experienced war, the killing of humanity, and the destruction of entire villages and once fertile land—it all softened my heart and my ego.

One Memorial Day weekend, decades later, I happened to be in Orlando visiting my father. Saturday afternoon I took dad to the Orlando Executive Airport to see a World War II B17 bomber. It was flown in for Memorial Day. Dad was now in his eighties but had no difficulty climbing the small ladder to enter the aircraft. He had some interesting stories about test flights of these bombers when he was in North Africa. I was somewhat amazed how small the fuselage was compared to the overall size of this plane with its massive wings and four large Pratt & Whitney radial engines. As we walked back to our car, I asked Dad if he enjoyed seeing this now vintage airplane. He said "Yep, you bet."

The following day, Sunday, I rose early to go for coffee and to fuel my car in preparation to head back to Tennessee. After filling my tank, the display on the screen informed me to see the attendant for a receipt.

I walked inside and the lone Asian attendant greeted me with a smile. Since it was early, I was the only customer, so I had the opportunity to ask if he had lost loved ones in war. I went on to share my sorrow for lives lost, especially my uncle who died at the Battle of the Bulge during World War II. As he handed me the receipt, he shared that he lost his mother and brother during the bombing of the city of Hanoi in North Vietnam in 1970. I was taken back. I told him that in 1970, I was a helicopter door gunner in the Mekong Delta region of South Vietnam. He told me he was in the North Vietnamese army and his duties were to build temporary bridges at night because the main bridges were destroyed by American bombs. Here were two men in their sixties that were once considered enemies at age nineteen, having a heartfelt conversation about war. We were once soldiers, fighting for a cause we believed in at the time, now questioning the absurdity of war and mourning for the men and women who lost lives due to it.

One evening I came upon a documentary about the Vietnam War and its effect on the children. After watching the well-made documentary, I thought of my granddaughter Autumn. In Autumn, I saw the innocence, the same innocence I saw in the faces of those Vietnamese children. What have their lives become? I had some contact with children in Vietnam, most often when we were shut down and out in the countryside waiting for a mission. It seems that every time we landed and shut the engine down, even in the most isolated or remote places, children would appear. It was never clear where they came from, but there they were.

One young boy about ten or twelve hobbled up to our helicopter on a homemade wooden crutch under one arm and a coconut cradled like a football in the other. He lost his leg just above the knee from a landmine. I don't remember how he opened the coconut, but he shared it with our crew. I found it good and tasted nothing like the coconut sprinkled on top of a cake that I've never cared for. We usually always had to keep an eye on the children because some would steal. They were most interested in food or things they could sell. By the looks of these children it was mainly for survival. We kept them away from the machine guns, ammunition, smoke canisters, hand grenades, and personal arms but would give them rations if we had extras. It was somewhat hard for them to steal anything of size because they usually only had on a tattered loose fitting lightweight shirt and shorts. As I sit here and think back, those children were polite, cordial, and usually had smiles on their faces even though they must have lived in fear. The younger the child the healthier and whiter their teeth; as they grew older, their teeth began to discolor and eventually fall out in later years. Being peasants, they were most likely too poor to even have a pair of sandals, so as they grew older, their feet and toes would spread wider and wider.

I was once asked about the movie *Platoon*. Oliver Stone, the director and combat infantry veteran, tried to interject as much as possible in a one-year tour of an infantry soldier and his platoon. I never had it as bad as the infantry when it came to physical hardship. Mental anguish is much more prevalent in soldiers who experienced combat. I can only speak for myself and my experiences. I can remember things that happened that didn't seem right, or something inside of me felt this was wrong, but I didn't understand enough to take a stand one way or another.

One example that comes to mind is the evacuation of a small village in the Mekong Delta region. Our helicopters and infantry soldiers had just destroyed a small hamlet, killed some suspected Vietcong, and burnt their small village to the ground. Something about destroying a village by setting it ablaze, just because we encountered enemy soldiers or gun fire, didn't seem right. The US policy at that time was to destroy any village that may have helped the Vietcong. But most of the inhabitants were women, children, and the elderly. The young men were off either fighting for South or for North Vietnam. That village may have stood for a hundred or more years up to that point, and the surrounding rice paddies was their whole life. It had supported many generations, and now it no longer exists.

After the battle, we extracted the soldiers and returned them to their base of operation. After all the helicopters unloaded the last remaining troops, we were ordered to fly back to the smoldering village. As we got closer and started to descend, I saw the smoke from the village hanging in the humid air. Of the six or so helicopters in the flight, I was the door gunner on the last helicopter. We were directed to land on a rice paddy dike, a mound of dirt that separated one rice paddy from another, in a straight line, one helicopter behind the other. We were told not to shut down, to keep power to the rotor blades.

It wasn't long when I noticed Vietnamese, mainly older women and small children with their mothers, walking towards us. As they got closer, they were being directed to board the helicopters and as a group got closer to our helicopter I could see they were very apprehensive. This may have been the first time my heart stirred with compassion for the Vietnamese people. I stood outside the helicopter next to my small canvas seat, my machine gun lying on the floor where, in flight, I kept my feet. With my flight helmet on and sun visor down they couldn't see my eyes, but I could see theirs. I could see the anxiety in their dark eyes. They probably had never been this close to a helicopter, though they saw them daily. Up close there was the noise of the engine, the rotor blades washing them with wind and debris, and the smell of burnt jet fuel, and they were being told to climb aboard and sit on a rough, dirty aluminum floor littered with spent cartridges. There were no seats, nothing to hold on to, and no doors to protect them from falling out. What made things worse was the dike wasn't quite wide enough to accommodate a helicopter, so they had to maneuver through the brown muddy water of the rice paddy, placing them about a foot below the skids. I helped them climb aboard. One child had a bag of rice, another carried the rice pot, and another member had a few clothes tied in a ball. This may have been the only material possessions that survived or all they could quickly retrieve before being forced to evacuate. During the boarding process, they huddled tightly together. Extended family wanted to of course stay together. This became somewhat of a problem because we only had so much room, plus weight is a factor for takeoff, especially in the afternoon heat and humidity.

The pilot keyed the radio and told Jon and me that some passengers had to get off and go to another helicopter because we were overloaded. This is always hard to do because we didn't speak Vietnamese, and they certainly didn't understand why some would need to get off. But, in time, we managed to lighten the load so we could get airborne. As we increased power and started to lift off, I scanned our wary passengers, and they were truly scared. But they held their loved ones tightly as we bounced side to side and up and down gradually gaining altitude. These poor souls also had to endure riding in the "trail position," or the last helicopter in the flight. Because of the narrow landing and takeoff area, we would have to stay in a straight line until we got to an altitude where we could fly in a V formation. When flying "trail" and staying in a straight line, the pilot has to fly in the rotor wash and hot exhaust of the helicopters in front of him, making for a very bumpy ride even for seasoned flyers. The smell of burnt JP-4 jet fuel filled the turbulent air with a toxic odor, a most unpleasant ride for our new passengers. As we formed into the V, our ride did settle down, but we didn't stay in the formation long before we started to descend.

We landed at a facility that looked to me like a refugee camp or, sad to say, like a concentration camp. Barbed wire and fencing surrounded the entire perimeter, and two wooden gates were guarded by South Vietnamese soldiers. As I assisted some of our passengers off the helicopter, they sought out other family members, and then, as a group, they walked toward the opening gates. Again, something stirred inside of my heart, and as they walked with their backs to me, I wondered briefly what their lives would be like. I didn't see one turn back to look, nor did I expect them to. What good had we done for them? Do they remember the young slim door gunner, dressed in the olive drab flight suit and dark flight helmet? I remember them and can still see some of their faces, especially a mother and her young daughter holding each other in tight embrace.

During my block of time in the army, Lieutenant Calley was on trial for war crimes at My Lai in South Vietnam. I wasn't aware of what happened until I came home, though I wasn't surprised. I had seen injustice and abuse but never to the extent of what happened in My Lai. I do remember quite vividly inserting ARVN, South Vietnam army soldiers, into a small village. The soldiers I encountered were not aggressive, not at all trained professional soldiers. They rarely engaged the enemy and it seemed they knew there wasn't any danger in the areas we inserted them. When they exited the helicopter they would sometimes walk upright, as if they knew the enemy wasn't around. They wouldn't scramble for cover, staying low like American soldiers. After a while I had a feeling within my gut that some insertions were not necessary. This was more of a show. The South Vietnamese soldiers, and, I think, most civilians, weren't too concerned about winning this war.

On this particular insertion we were told the village was a free fire zone, meaning we could shoot into the village, killing anyone or, for some door gunners, if given the chance, dogs, pigs, or even water buffalos. Anyone in the village was considered Vietcong. Because of the terrain and the landing location we had to fly fairly low, staying in a straight line about 10 to 15 feet off the ground. This took us right in front of and parallel to this village, approximately 30 feet from the huts. It was like driving down the main street of a small American town shooting into their buildings. This village was like most: flimsy huts with straw roofs. Our helicopter was toward the end of the string of about seven or eight. As we came in, more as a hover than as a fast approach, the commander said, "Your door gunners can open up." I sat at the ready, my machine gun held securely in my arms, but I didn't fire. I was cautious and had my finger on the trigger but was quite certain it wasn't necessary. A part of me argued with myself that by shooting, I'd put wear and tear on the gun that may be needed for a legitimate firefight. Also, I felt no enemy combatants were in the village, and if civilians were hiding inside their paper-thin structures, the bullets from this high-powered machine gun could easily find them. I also knew my tracer rounds, every fifth bullet in the linked ammunition, could ignite the structures. I was correct in my assumption that this insertion of troops was going to be unproductive and unnecessary. To my knowledge, no human lives were taken, but I'm afraid war has a way of producing an ugly side of humanity that can escalate into a My Lai incident.

. . .

I received my orders to return home a few weeks before my official one-year date. President Nixon was pulling down the troop levels and, since I was somewhat short, I was included. I mailed most of my personal effects home to my parents so I could travel light. I was fortunate to get a ride to the 90th Replacement Battalion at Long Binh from a colonel who was getting in some flight hours in a OH-6 Cayuse, nicknamed "Loach." He was happy to personally transport a fellow helicopter crew member. I had never flown on this type of helicopter nor in the copilot's seat, so it was an experience to remember. The four-rotor blade Loach was very fast and maneuverable, with a distinctly different sound than the UH1 Huey I was familiar with. Upon landing I thanked the colonel. He gave me a smile and said good luck.

With my small personal bag in one hand and my captured Vietcong rifle slung over my shoulder, I walked maybe 50 yards to the gate. As I got close to the short dirt road that led off the main road, I saw to my right a Vietnamese woman in her fifties squatting in the tall grass relieving herself. I looked with disgust; and I know I projected that to her. It's a moment I look back on and feel truly ashamed. I had spent almost a year in her country yet never thought in-depth about the daily lives of Vietnamese civilians.

After entering the center, I gathered with other soldiers processing out. We were told to remove our jungle fatigues and throw them in large open bins. A third bin was for our jungle boots, but we were given the option to take them home if we wanted to keep them.

My captured rifle had all the necessary paperwork in order to take it home as a war souvenir. The rifle was a 1960 bolt action Chinese type 53 carbine. The rifle, and numerous others, were captured at the end of April 1970, when we invaded Cambodia. I wanted to give it to my father. And after my father passed in 2017, I wanted to donate it to a Vietnam War archive or a military weapons museum. I thought I would include this letter with it:

. . .

Dear Vietnam War Archive,

I would like to include some history of the 1960 Chinese Type 53 carbine rifle. As you can see, it's old, tattered, and part of the stock is missing. When we invaded Cambodia in April of 1970, this rifle along with many other captured weapons were loaded on helicopters and brought back to our base camp. Only rifles that were not fully automatic could be brought home to the States as war trophies. "War trophy" is the term used on the DD Form 603-1 that had to accompany the rifle to its destination. I wanted to give it to my father. Now that he has passed, I would like your archives to have it.

The rifle was filthy and based on its appearance probably saw combat the entire first ten years of its existence. When having it registered and authorized to be taken back to the States, it did need to be cleaned up before it could be approved. I wanted to leave it as it was found but knowing the dirt and mud had to be removed, I used a small wire brush to lightly remove the grime. Since the front forearm stock was partially missing and splintered, I used a file to round over any sharp edges. My desire was to give it to my father but only as a war souvenir, never to have another round fired from its barrel. In fact, as tattered as it is, I would be afraid to shoot it.

Until I finished out my tour, the rifle would be secured in the arms room. When I received orders to return home, I showed the orders to the arms room sergeant to retrieve the rifle.

Before I could board the Freedom Bird, the commercial airliner that would take me home, I had to remove the bolt and keep it in my carry-on bag. The rifle was then placed in the baggage compartment.

I did have one problem with my flight home and that was at our first stop to refuel and, I think, changeout crew members. They told us we had to disembark the aircraft while it was refueled and it would take about thirty to forty minutes. They also stressed when the call came to board that we were to move quickly to the gate and that if you're not on the plane when they made the final call, they'd leave you.

While we were in the terminal the military police had their drug-sniffing dog walk through the aircraft. They randomly picked a carry-on bag to stash a bag of drugs. This was to reward the dog if no other drugs were found. They selected my bag to plant the drugs. When opening the bag, they saw the bolt and felt it was contraband. I was ordered to report to the military police counter, and it took a while for them to confirm the bolt was from my war trophy. I was getting concerned they weren't going to get this straightened out before the last call to board, but it was finally resolved, though I was the last one to board.

After many hours of flight, we landed at Fort Dix New Jersey, where I was discharged. The army took us by bus to the local airport. In the terminal, no one noticed or seem to care I had a rifle slung over my shoulder. As I boarded an Eastern Airlines flight to Orlando, the flight attendant said she would secure the rifle in the tall closet at the front of the plane. I found my seat and settled in. I had a strong feeling the man sitting two seats from me was the air marshal assigned to the flight. I wasn't bothered if he or the flight crew felt they needed to keep an eye on me. After landing, the crew had me wait until all passengers were off the plane before they'd hand me the rifle.

This rifle that most likely saw ten hard years of service, hung on the wall of my father's den for the next forty-eight years.

As I ready it to be sent to you, I can't help but feel sorrow for all who handled this rifle as well as those who were killed or wounded by it. I held it to my shoulder and looked through the sights, wondering what enemy soldiers might have held it the same way, their cheek resting on this rough stock, eyes lining up their target.
—*Bill Schmitzer*

. . .

The flight home was like my arrival, very long but the uncertainty of what was in store for my yearlong tour was no longer an issue. While it took my father and Uncle Roy over two weeks by boat to return home from World War II, it took me a daylong flight.

We landed at Fort Dix New Jersey in the late afternoon to grey skies with light rain and cold temperatures. That evening, I enjoyed a hot meal and a warm shower. The next day involved processing out. I was given a physical, had my teeth checked and given a dress uniform. That same afternoon some of us were loaded on a military bus and driven to a civilian airport to head home. I remember walking through the airport in my dress uniform, with my jungle boots slung over my bag and a tattered rifle slung over my shoulder. The Vietnam War was still raging and the airport was filled with military personnel, so no one seemed to take special notice of me. As I boarded the aircraft, a flight attendant said she would secure the rifle in a garment closet. I found my window seat and it felt good to sit and relax for a while. Just as we were getting ready to taxi, a fairly large man sat in the aisle seat two seats from me. I had a feeling the flight's air marshal was keeping an eye on me.

I arrived home late in the evening. I had heard reports of war protesters harassing returning veterans, but I didn't see any at either airport. When I arrived at my parents' house, I saw a large sign taped to the garage door that said, "Welcome home, Bill!"

The next evening my mother and grandmother fixed a wonderful meal: a large juicy baked ham; asparagus; rolls; and my mother's homemade potato salad that she knew I loved. She also knew I enjoyed her pies, so she made a pecan, cherry, and chocolate pie. Uncle Roy was also there for the meal. He and I would kiddingly fight over mom's potato salad. It was nice to sit down with loving family for a warm, comforting meal and good conversation. It was also nice to no longer be in Vietnam and to be officially out of the army. I'd never considered a career in the army—I was a hometown boy. Being in the military meant moving from place to place.

. . .

Now that I was home I had to report to my local army reserve unit and give the commander my records. I was drafted for six years but only had to serve two of those years in active duty. The last four would be as a reservist. Since I was sent to Vietnam, I would not be required to attend monthly weekend reserve meetings. Though, if necessary, during those four years, I could be called up for active duty. I elected not to attend meetings; I was through with the military and hopefully war.

. . .

I was eventually hired by the Orlando Fire Department and spent twenty-five years in a most rewarding career. I did know a few Vietnam veterans who were also in the department. During my firefighting career, I didn't talk too much about Vietnam. I did have one incident in my thirties when Vietnam raised its head, so to speak. One afternoon, I was volunteering at a high school swim meet when an isolated thunderstorm moved in. As many parents and coaches opened colorful umbrellas or slipped into fluorescent rain gear, I donned a twenty-one-year-old Vietnam poncho. While standing there, rain pelting the heavy plastic, I overheard a student comment how ugly my tattered olive-green poncho was.

The next morning as I sipped on a cup of coffee, I thought of what that high school senior said. If only he knew what that old poncho represented, so much more than a mere raincoat. I thought back to when I was a senior at that very high school. Little did I know that in less than a year, I would be drafted and sent to Vietnam.

. . .

I read a book about a twenty-seven-year-old female doctor who was in the North Vietnamese Army. Her field hospital, probably considered quite primitive to our MASH units, was hidden in the dense jungle. I'm sure American helicopters had flown over and around her hospital numerous times not knowing it was beneath them. She was killed in 1970 by an American infantry company. She served at that hospital for three years, dedicating her life to saving others' lives and fighting for a cause she believed in. In her journal, that later became a book, I don't remember her mentioning anything spiritual. Many Vietnamese believed in Buddhism but there were also Christians. I wonder if she believed in a higher power. I've often heard in American Christianity that salvation is only offered through the blood of Jesus and only those who believe in him will be saved. I do believe that he did die for all humanity, so I wonder about this young doctor or the Vietcong soldier lying face down in the muddy rice paddy. What about them? I certainly didn't know them spiritually, but they could have been more caring, and have had more compassion and love for their fellow man than I or people confessing to be Christian. Does God recognize their existence? I sure hope he does, and will also deal justly with all, no matter what they believe.

. . .

I don't know if I learned this when I was in the service because I can re-member having compassion for the underdog, the unfortunate, or those folks that are being mistreated. Maybe it's because I was laughed at or made fun of when I was in school. I didn't fully understand why I was bothered when one of my classmates were being picked on or made to feel small but seeing the Vietnamese being abused and mistreated made it perfectly clear just how mean and unjust humanity can be. My tour taught me that these people weren't inferior or less than; they were hu-man beings just like me with the same desire for love, acceptance, and equal treatment. I often think about the impoverished Vietnamese, who are likely still living with dirt floors in their crude huts and barely exist-ing from farming rice. Their land was contaminated by Agent Orange, causing premature deaths or children born with birth defects, and they never know when a left-behind landmine just a step away might detonate, causing the loss of limb or death.

Out of my two years of active service I would say what was most life-changing was my spiritual awakening. One evening we were flying the Nighthawk mission and were shut down in a clearing waiting for orders. I had been in Vietnam for a while and was no longer considered a "newbie." It was just getting dark, and the mosquitoes were starting to bite. Vietnam, for me, was such an eerie place at night. As the other three crew members huddled up talking, I sat on the aluminum floor with my feet dangling outside. I stared down at the dull-green, sharply pointed grass. I thought about what a senseless war this was. To die on this soil was heart wrenching, not only for me but also for civilians and all brothers in arms, that would include the enemy. I wondered if there was something more than just living a block of time on this earth and then dying. I want to believe there is. For many, life is filled with injustice, heartache, and pain. I hope for those folks something better is waiting for them after this life. As for me, I hope for the same, but if not, well, I'm content and comforted believing in that hope.

. . .

One final thought. Now that I'm a senior, I've had the opportunity to study the history of Vietnam, to learn about the men and women who fought for control of their small country from before World War II until after America was defeated. I've wondered if the killing, destruction, and expense could have been avoided if only those in power at the time would have met on neutral ground, discussed their grievances, leader to leader, and strived to find a solution to their differences. Has that ever been done? Is it possible?

Orlando Fire Department

In early 1971, when I had just returned from Vietnam, I ran into a long-time friend of my parents in the tool department at Sears. He expressed this happiness that I'd returned home safely and asked what I had planned to do next. I told him I wasn't sure. I didn't share with him that I didn't feel compelled to work at my parents' meat market. He asked me, "Have you considered the city of Orlando police or fire department?"

I thought for a moment and said, "No." I knew I wouldn't be interested in the police department, and told him as much, so he suggested I may want to look into the fire department. He had been a fireman with the city and liked it but had an opportunity to move into a higher paying job in a different department. He said I may want to check it out.

I thanked him for the idea and went home and told my mother and father. They seemed fine with the idea and never let on if they were disappointed that I didn't want to work for them. I know they would be happy if at some point I would take over their business they'd worked so hard to build. Dad said, "You know, Vernon is a fireman." Vernon Thomas was the barber who'd been cutting my hairs since I was a kid. I remember going in for a haircut and seeing Vernon sitting in his barber chair studying a fire department street map. At that time, before you could be a permanent firefighter, you had to pass a street test that covered the entire city limits. Even though Orlando was a fairly small community in the 1950s, for anyone to learn all the streets was a big undertaking.

One morning I drove the six or so blocks to the fire station that housed Engine 4. I walked through the large bay door, past Engine 4, a 1950s Seagrave, and into the kitchen area. I was kindly greeted by the four crewmen on shift that day. I shared my interest in the fire department and was interested in what it's like being a fireman. The driver of the truck took me out to the apparatus floor to show me the truck, equipment used for fighting fires as well as their personal equipment. I knew very little about the fire department. My knowledge and understanding was limited to the following: the truck was painted red, and it carried both a hose to extinguish a fire and a ladder, which was attached to its side. I didn't know the truck had a water tank and pump to propel the water through the hose and out the nozzle. I had no idea how this all worked.

The driver, or engineer, was very helpful and encouraged me to pursue more. He told me I would first have to take a civil service test. If I passed that, I would take a physical and mental examination. I went to city hall to obtain information about the civil service test and when it would be given. I signed up for the next test. The test was given in the cafeteria at city hall on a Wednesday night at 7:00. When I arrived, the facilitator asked which test I wanted to take, "Fire or police?" I said fire department and he gave me a copy of the test. I found a table and sat down. We had to keep the test booklet closed until the facilitator told us to start. We only had so much time to complete the test, and I was the last to finish before they called the end time. My slow reading and my challenges with reading comprehension were what took me so long to finish. With everyone gone except for me and the facilitator, I quietly waited for him to grade my test. As I looked on, I could see him making red x's next to the questions I missed. I could tell I wasn't doing well and hoped I didn't miss so many that I failed. It turned out that I did fail. I could tell the facilitator, who was just a little older than me, felt bad. I failed by only one point. He immediately said how sorry he was but encouraged me to take it again and believed I would pass next time. I was bummed but decided to take it again soon. In the meantime, I got a job with Jordan Marsh department store as a stock clerk. A month later, I had the opportunity to take the test again, and this time I passed.

Soon afterwards I was contacted by the City of Orlando for an appointment for a physical and psychological evaluation, both of which I passed. In June of 1971, I started my career with the Orlando Fire Department (OFD).

On my first day I was to report to Fire Station 1 on a Friday morning. Station 1 was located on Magnolia Avenue between South Street and Anderson Street. Built in 1960, it was fairly new as well as quite large for the time. Three stories high, with a mezzanine and five deep apparatus bays, some of the older veterans referred to it as "headquarters" because it housed the different sections of the department. Communications/dispatch was on the first floor behind the apparatus bays, with a large picture window looking out over the bays (I had heard the glass was bulletproof). Running parallel to the bay floor, the chief of the department and his secretary had private offices as well as the two deputy chiefs. Their office windows also looked out at the apparatus floor.

On the second floor was a mezzanine above the chiefs' offices that looked down over the bay floor and fire equipment. That floor had offices for fire prevention, arson investigation, the photographer, the cartographer, and the supply section, which issued uniforms and turnout gear. Midway down the mezzanine was a fire pole for accessing the trucks quickly. A pipe guardrail protected anyone from accidentally stepping off, and you had to unclip a chain before you could slide down to the first floor. The third floor—directly over the apparatus floor—housed the dormitory. It was outfitted with forty-eight Murphy beds that folded up into the wall, and wooden floor-to-ceiling lockers. Four fire poles, symmetrically placed throughout the dorm to quickly access the bay floor whenever a call came in. There were also a few individual bedrooms for shift chiefs, a large classroom, and two conference rooms with large wooden pocket doors that could be slid open to create a larger classroom setting.

As I walked through the front door on that first morning, I noticed all kinds of fire equipment and tools sitting on the concrete apron in front of the station, and upon entering the office, Fay Craig, secretary to the chief, greeted me. She was pleasant and professional and had me sit in a chair across from her desk. In front of her her electric IBM typewriter, she rolled in two employment forms, carbon paper sandwiched between them. As I answered her questions her fingers rapidly typed the information on the forms. She had a large picture window that faced the apparatus floor. While sitting there I noticed all the fire equipment had been pulled out onto the front apron, firemen with brooms and metal mop buckets were sweeping and mopping the reddish-brown tile floor. When all forms were complete, Fay gave me the address for the training grounds at Station 6 where I was to report for training.

Since Station 6 was at the Orlando Municipal Airport, it also housed a small crash truck. When I was a small child, my mother once took me to this airport to pick up my father from a Chicago flight. (The Orlando Municipal Airport would later be renamed the Orlando Executive Airport. The Orlando International Airport did not yet exist.)

I drove to Station 6 and found the training building. I walked up a few wooden steps, through the wooden door into a small classroom. Hearing the door open, Captain Elmer Martin greeted me. After introductions, Captain Martin took me outside to a fire hydrant and taught me how to pull hose from the back of an old fire truck and hook it to a fire hydrant. He also showed me how to don and breathe through a self-contained breathing apparatus. That was the extent of my training at that time. I was told to have lunch and at 1:00 p.m. report back to Station 1 for the rest of the shift. This shift would last until 8:00 a.m. the next morning.

Back at Station 1, the captain on duty told me I would be riding in the jump seat behind the driver on Engine 51. I was loaned a fire coat and helmet, both taken from the numerous coats and helmets hanging from hooks on the south wall on the apparatus floor (three-quarter rubber fire boots were not yet being issued). Afterwards, Dean, the driver of Engine 51, gave me a tour of the truck and firehouse. We got as far as the dormitory where Dean was going to show me how to slide the fire pole, when a loud bell rang. Over the station's radio we listened to the list of apparatus to respond and the address of the emergency. Dean stepped out onto the fire pole and wrapped his legs around it. But before he started to slide, he said, "Don't hold too tight with your hands or you'll get a blister." I wrapped my legs on the pole as he showed me and started down, quite surprised at how fast I began to slide. My instinct was to tighten up on the pole with my hands, Dean was correct, I received a sizable blister on the palm of one hand.

I made it down the pole, threw on my borrowed fire coat, and climbed aboard. I scooted back in the jump seat so my back rested against the breathing apparatus. I remember the deep powerful sound coming from the Detroit Diesel engine under the metal cowling next to me. I was amazed at how fast the truck accelerated. It seemed like we left the apparatus bay going at least 50 miles an hour. When Dean turned north on Magnolia Avenue and upshifted, I thought we may take off from the ground. Facing backwards I felt as if I was being pulled toward the back of the apparatus from the sheer speed of the truck. With air horns blasting and windup sirens wailing, I was experiencing my first fire response—or "run" as it was typically called.

Turning to look forward I saw another fire engine ahead of us, and behind us was a ladder truck, a rescue truck, and a chief's car. I struggled to work my arms into the shoulder straps of the breathing apparatus, or air pack. I then slipped the mask strap over my neck, letting the mask dangle in my lap, I then secured the MSA polycarbonate fire helmet on top of my head. As we flew up Magnolia Avenue, I looked out the side window to watch cars and pedestrians coming to a stop as we whizzed by. As we got close to Robinson Street, I felt the engine starting to brake. After making the right turn onto Robinson, Dean downshifted and once again we quickly accelerated, though this was short-lived as we pulled next to the fire hydrant on the corner of Robinson Street and Rosalind Avenue. We were suddenly on the scene of some type of fire at the Hartford Insurance Company building. The lieutenant turned in his seat and told the firefighter sitting behind him, "We're going to lay into the system." Since this was a high-rise building the second due engine would automatically lay two dry hose lines into the building's standpipe system. The engine would then hook up to the hydrant using the black, hard, suction hose—6 inches in diameter and 10 feet long—which rides on a tray on the side of the fire truck. I had found I had to pull myself forward with some force to overcome the clamping action that held the air pack secure in its bracket. Climbing down I headed to the rear of the truck, after turning the corner

I saw two 2½-inch hose lines being pulled, thrown, and stretched to the building. I somewhat knew what the objective was but was apprehensive on how to help. We soon heard over the lieutenant's portable radio that it was an alarm malfunction; there was no emergency. We now only had to reload the hose and returned to the firehouse. This would be my first ever emergency run, the one run every firefighter remembers.

The rest of my tour was uneventful. We had supper that evening and slept the entire night without responding to another alarm. I was relieved around 7:30 the next morning and made sure I returned the borrowed coat and helmet to its original location. Before I left for my two days off, I was told to report to Firehouse 7 on Monday morning. I would be assigned to Engine 7 until enough new personnel were hired to form a training class.

. . .

Station 7 was a fairly new station with two apparatus bays, each bay long enough to park two engines, one behind the other. At that time there were two engines being housed there, Engine 7 and Engine 10. The long-term plans for the fire department were to build another fire station to house Engine 10. This was to cover the area annexed by the city that was being rapidly built up with hotels in anticipation of Disney World's arrival.

Also at that time the city had purchased a new Sutphen tower ladder, which was being housed at Station 7. This truck would replace the old tiller ladder truck at Station 1 and remain at Station 7 until all crew members assigned to Ladder 1 were familiar with the tower ladder. Engine 10 was moved behind Engine 7 and the tower ladder was parked in the adjoining bay. We were responsible for cleaning the truck after a day of training. I was somewhat interested in this apparatus but didn't know why at the time.

There were a couple things I didn't care for at Station 7. The entire station was kept locked at all times with an 8-foot chain-link fence and a foot or more of barbed wire above that to keep vandals from breaking into the station and personal cars. Since I had recently returned home from Vietnam, I found this unsettling. One other disappointment I encountered was the number of practical jokes that occurred on a regular basis. I understood I was the newbie and would be the brunt of these jokes, but the pranks were childish and constant. I didn't see any professionalism and wondered if I had made a mistake. I wasn't in the same situation as I was when I was drafted into the army; I had the option to quit and pursue another endeavor. But my only other option at the time was to work as a butcher at the meat market. I knew I wouldn't be content working in that field for thirty to forty years. When I received my first paycheck from the fire department, I was pleasantly surprised. I was hired in the middle of the two-week pay cycle so the next Friday, I received my first paycheck for $105.53. That was about the same amount my monthly pay was in the army.

I was uncomfortable not knowing what was expected of me, what my job would be if we had a fire or first aid call. In Vietnam I was fortunate to have my crew chief, Jon, to teach me what my duties were. I wish the captain of Engine 7, or even the engineer, would give me some guidance. I did ask the captain what I was to do if we had a fire, and he said he would tell me when we arrived on the scene, but I wasn't reassured. I would learn later that the Orlando Fire department didn't have any standard operating procedures (SOPs) at that time.

One strange chore that was required after we returned the apparatus to quarters was to wipe the truck clean, including the truck's wheel wells. Some engineers used a flashlight to inspect the cleaning, and if it wasn't done to his approval, it was cleaned again. I understood that the apparatus was the pride of the fire service and was to be kept bright and shiny at all times, but the wheel wells? One other duty the newest person was required to do was clean the oil drip pans under the apparatus. These flat metal pans, about 3' x 4', could be wiped with a rag if the truck didn't leak oil or fluids too rapidly. If the water tank leaked, it made for more of a mess. Sometimes it was easier to slide the pans out from underneath the trucks and lay them on the front apron of the station, sprinkle them with comet cleaner, scrub them with a brush, and hose them off. Back then there wasn't a concern where these fluids flowed to.

On Saturday, "truck day," they got an even more thorough cleaning, like a coat of paste wax and an inventory of its equipment. Every piece of equipment from a pencil in the glove box to a fire nozzle attached to the tail board was listed in the three-ring binder kept in the cab of the truck. Firefighter L.J. Smith, who was also a crew member, would read down the list of items, I'd confirm they were physically there, and he would put a check in the box next to that item. Since L.J. had been on the job a few months longer than me and had gone through a training class I often asked him questions. He was very intelligent, kindhearted, and treated me with respect. We often cooked and ate together because the rest of the crews at this firehouse did not. L.J. also served a tour as a marine in Vietnam. He was my first friend in the department, and we stayed close throughout our careers. (L.J. unfortunately died in 2013 at the age of sixty-five from cancer.)

L.J. and I responded together to my first call for first aid, the call every firefighter remembers. The call came in as "a cutting" at a small apartment complex behind the station. We turned left out of the station, a left at the next street, and another left at the next street. When we arrived, I grabbed the first aid box and followed the lieutenant and L.J. inside of the small ground-floor apartment. A party was going on with loud music and wall-to-wall people. Two girls signaled us to a small bathroom where a young teenage girl was bleeding from both of her wrists. Since I had the first aid box, and the bathroom was very small, L.J. and I entered with the young victim and one of her friends. We don't know if she had cut herself or someone else did the cutting, but she had a deep cut on top of each wrist reaching down to the bone. These weren't life threatening, in fact there wasn't too much blood, but the wounds would definitely need stitches. We placed a couple of small square pads and wrapped her wrists with Kling dressing to cover the wounds. The young girl was calm and didn't say a word. An ambulance arrived, and we turned her over to them.

One Saturday I was assigned to ride Engine 10. That afternoon we received a call for a trash fire at a high-rise hotel under construction on International Drive. Upon arrival the trash fire was confined to discarded building materials, such as lumber, cardboard, and wooden pallets. The fire was a fair distance from the structure. Engine 10 stopped upwind of the fire. The lieutenant told us to use two booster lines to put the fire out. The engineer shifted the truck into pump and I and the other firefighter each grabbed a Hardi pistol-type nozzle attached to a solid black hose that reminded me of a large-diameter garden hose. Each of these high-pressure, low-volume hoses were wrapped on their own reels. We would hopefully extinguish the fire before we emptied, at that time, the 300-gallon water tank.

This afternoon was unusually windy, and this wind was making the fire grow, plus it was lifting some of the light cardboard boxes and sending them flaming toward the building. The lieutenant and engineer were staying busy stomping them out. We weren't making much headway, plus the engineer was concerned we were going to run out of water before the fire could be extinguished. It wasn't long before I was told to hand-lay a 2½-inch supply hose line to a hydrant about 150 feet away. We now had an unlimited water supply and, in time, extinguished the fire. What was dispatched as a rubbish fire almost got out of control. That fire was my first official fire but maybe because this fire was outside and not inside of a structure it didn't end up having the same impact that my first run or first aid emergency had. I think I was still wondering what a structure fire would be like, to advance a hose line into a burning structure, then to locate, confine, and extinguish it. I would have to wait on that one.

. . .

When enough recruits were hired we came off shift and assembled on a Monday morning at the training division of the Orlando Fire Department. I believe the buildings and training tower were built by the air force during World War II. There were around twenty-five males, and no females, in the class. Some had been to college; firefighter Jan Witengier had gone to the University of Florida. The training class would take place from Monday to Friday, eight hours a day, for eight weeks. A typical day would begin with station cleanup of Firehouse 6, then physical exercise, and then a morning run. Our run took us down and back along a taxi way. The rest of the morning was classroom work involving the study of the science of fire, first aid, search and rescue, different types of hose and ladders, ropes and knots, salvage operations, different kinds of breathing apparatuses, etc. After lunch was usually outside work at the hydrant and tower involving hose evolutions and raising different types and lengths of ground ladders. We took written tests every Friday mornings, I found I had to study quite hard to make Cs and really hard to make Bs. I envied those in my class that were quite smart, easily retained the information, and didn't have to put in hours of study. The instructors were able to smoke up the training tower by building a fire in an open 55-gallon drum. This would keep the fire contained to the drum, but the smoke produced would fill the enclosed parts of the tower. At that time the instructors would build fires with whatever they could find, wood products, cardboard, hay, or straw, but who knows what was thrown in. I was told later that PVC pipe was added to produce dense black smoke. We hadn't understood the danger of breathing such toxic chemicals at the time. There weren't enough MSA breathing apparatuses to go around, so we had to use smoke masks that weren't the best at filtering smoke, and I often went home with a headache.

If I remember correctly, along with a written test, we had two tasks we must accomplish to graduate. The first was to jump into a round net 8 feet in diameter held by eight recruits. This jump was from the roof of the second story, about 20 feet, though it seemed much higher when you were looking down at the net below. You were to jump out over the net and lie backwards, this would position your fall to hopefully land flat on your back. It was very unnatural to do and took having a great deal of confidence in those holding the net. They held it with their arms flexed, the metal rim of the net positioned at their upper chest right below their neck, and hands facing toward each recruit. As the person made contact with the net, those holding the net would extend their arms down, absorbing the fall. Ideally, if you landed in the middle of the net, the recruits would simply bend their arms downwards at the elbows making for a fairly comfortable landing. This was definitely the safest for the jumper and those holding the net; the load would be distributed equally among all the recruits, so as not to injure anyone. You only had to jump once to pass and that was enough for some.

The other task each member must accomplish was to raise a straight ladder 30 feet long made entirely of wood. This ladder was extremely heavy, so those who were taller and had above average strength had an easier time with it. The ladder was laid flat with the butt of the ladder up against the wall of the wooden training tower. You then went to the opposite end, picked up the ladder and pushed it above your head, then walked hand over hand each rung to raise the ladder against the building. The ladder was heavy, which is where strength came in but also the height of the recruit acted as a fulcrum. One thing I did notice was when doing ladder work some recruits were very uncomfortable with heights. Some never overcame this fear; hopefully, for their sake, they never encountered a situation during which they had to make a rescue, or operate, at an extreme height.

There were some outstanding recruits in my class. One was Paul Skinner, natural at just about everything. When climbing ladders, he made it look effortless, and he had no fear working at heights. Our class felt he would become the rising star, and he was. He quickly rose in rank, retiring many years later while an assistant chief. He also earned a master's degree in public administration from the University of Central Florida. As I now think back, most in our class did quite well and, after graduating, went on to become company officers; a few even became chiefs.

One morning during hose training centered around the fire hydrant, the new tower ladder arrived for training purposes at the training tower. We watched as Larry Camnitz, the deputy chief of combat, positioned this new apparatus parallel to the training tower, about 30 feet from the building. Walking over to greet the deputy chief was the assistant chief of training Bud Jackson, as well as another man. I don't recall who this man was—he may have been the Sutphen representative who delivered the tower ladder and was there to explain and train our department on their new investment. With the air brake applied the truck was set up for aerial operations. This entailed two hydraulic ground outrigger jacks, one on each side of the truck just behind the crew cab, that extended out from the apparatus about 4 feet. Another set of stabilization jacks were lowered behind each set of rear tandem wheels. With the truck raised and supported on these stabilization jacks, a hydraulic lever was moved to reroute the hydraulic fluid to operate the aerial boom.

The three men walked around to the rear of the apparatus and climbed up into the bucket. The aerial could now be operated from within the bucket. The deputy chief, working the controls, lifted the bucket upward out of the booms cradle and brought it up to its highest point, keeping the boom inline under the apparatus. It was then rotated ninety degrees to the right toward the tower. Once the "lower" lever and the "extension" lever were activated, the bucket started to make its way to the tower. What happened next happened in slow motion, with the weight of the boom plus its bucket and occupants, the ground beneath the left outrigger jack gave way. As this jack slowly sank into the asphalt the bucket slowly made its way to the ground. This caused the truck to tilt to its left side. With the bucket resting on the ground in front of the training tower, the apparatus was now resting on its left set of wheels, with its right-side wheels off the ground. Fortunately, no one was injured nor any major damage to the tower ladder.

I did not see how the truck was righted; we were back in the classroom by then. Luckily there was no major damage to this expensive fire apparatus. Though, to this day, you can still see ripples in the metal by sighting down the left side of the truck. To hopefully solve this problem from ever happening again, two support pads were fabricated from heavy corrugated aluminum, this was to keep the weight down but still give adequate support. These pads would be placed under each outrigger whenever the truck was set up for aerial operation. Two other smaller pads were made for the rear jacks as well.

As our training class progressed, I was getting more and more enthusiastic about the fire profession. Even though I didn't get a high score on the written tests, I felt I understood the subject. Where I did do well, at least in my eyes, was the practical, hands-on training. I liked how straight forward, methodical, step by step hose evolutions were performed. The more visual something was the better I understood it. Ladders were the same way. I had to study harder than most of my classmates when tested on the different parts that make up a ladder, but I felt comfortable raising and climbing them.

As time grew closer to graduation, we were asked if we had a preference in terms of which apparatus we would like to be assigned to. I requested Station 1. It was the busiest, and, it seemed to me, always had a lot going on. I felt it would be a good fit for me. I did not receive my request. I was sent to a slower company that didn't respond to many calls. But even this company was important to those residents in its response area. I wasn't bummed, as I understood since I most likely graduated in the middle of the class. I noticed that those who were at the top of the class did receive their request, and I felt that was fair. They did well and should be rewarded.

. . .

My first official company officer was Danny Rivenbark. He was friendly with a kind smile. My first duty was to learn the location of all equipment on the engine. In a fair amount of time, I could easily visualize every piece of equipment and where it was stored, similar to the visualization of the M60 machine gun. If I was told to get a certain nozzle, or the first aid box, or any tool, I could go directly to the correct compartment or location and retrieve it. I felt that was important, to be on an emergency scene and frantically searching one compartment after another for a tool or piece of equipment was not only unprofessional but could further endanger those we were there to help. I started to study a street map of our first and second response territory. I also studied for my permanent firefighter test that would come around in about a year. (I now use the word firefighter, not "fireman." There were rumors that the fire department was considering hiring females, so firefighter would become the acceptable title.)

We had fire related classes usually in the morning, but I was still extremely bored. We rarely left the station except for company inspection of buildings, and it was weeks between alarms.

Practical jokes and poking fun started soon after I arrived at the company. I may have done or said something that was incorrect, as one firefighter nicknamed me "Doofus." I didn't know what this word meant, but it didn't sound very respectful. It wasn't long before all members were calling me by this name, some even introducing me to their spouses by the name. I had learned from my short experience at Station 7 that harassing and poking fun at the new guy was part of the introduction into the fire service. But, for me, because I was laughed at and poked fun of most of my life, this bothered me more than most. In the dictionary, the word "doofus" refers to a stupid, incompetent, or foolish person. I'd always felt inferior due to my poor reading and spelling skills, but I wanted to feel I had other qualities that were also important; to be told you were stupid or incompetent or foolish was very hurtful to me. With this treatment continuing with no relief, I decided to address it with the crew members. One afternoon as everyone sat in the ready room, I addressed them and told them my feelings about being called a doofus. This caught some of the crew members off guard and they immediately understood and respected my feelings. But others didn't, and the abuse continued. I believe those that continued enjoyed making me feel small. I never said another word. I hoped I would gain their respect, and at some point, they would stop using the name. I had been thinking of requesting a transfer to Firehouse 1 and I certainly didn't want this nickname following me should I be granted the transfer.

Though my time at this firehouse wasn't entirely bad. Having Danny as my company officer was good. It would turn out that he would become a very influential person in my life. Danny is a spiritual man, and I liked that in him. Since I had a spiritual experience in Vietnam, we often sat on the wooden park bench in front of the firehouse and talked. Danny never pushed his denomination; we mainly talked about Jesus and his teachings when he walked this earth. I liked what Danny told me about that Jesus and how he represented justice, compassion, kindness, and, most of all, love for everyone. I was definitely attracted to this Jesus because I also wanted within my soul those same attributes. We had been talking frequently, and I could sense I was growing in my desire to better know and understand the teachings of Jesus.

One weekday afternoon in October, I had a desire to rest. To rest this time of day was uncharacteristic for me. I climbed the stairs to the dormitory and entered. The rest of the crew members were either in the ready room or in the kitchen preparing the evening meal.

The dormitory was fairly dark with only the late afternoon sun making its appearance between the closed blinds and the sides of the window frames. I laid down on my bed resting my head on the pillow, hands and forearms resting on my stomach, and closed my eyes. I felt I wanted to pray, but as in Vietnam I didn't know how to or what to even say. What came to mind was to tell God I too loved justice, compassion, kindness, and love. I also expressed my desire to become one of his followers.

What happened next was instantaneous, an extremely bright-white light appeared before my closed eyes accompanied by the not too loud sound of a horn. It only lasted three or four seconds. A comforting peacefulness seemed to flow throughout me. This peacefulness reminded me of when I stood at the doorway to Kimball's cubicle. I believe this white light and the sound of the horn was God's way of telling me he heard my prayer.

Had I just experienced being "born again," or "saved"? Up until this time, I was unfamiliar with those terms, yet after a while I came to understand the Christian definition of being saved or being born again. According to them, all a person had to do to be saved was to confess they believe in Jesus, and they would live with him for eternity after they die. That sounded all well and fine, but I was concerned about how to live a godly life from that moment forward until I did die. I knew I was a sinful man; I was ashamed of my past actions and felt I wasn't strong enough to fully live a godly life. My thoughts alone would disqualify me.

. . .

I now had two important interests, the fire department and spirituality. Though it was easy to see the fire department dominated the two. I started strong, studying and trying to learn as much as I could about those two areas, but in time the fire department would win, so to speak. My reading and study of the Bible was slowly declining and my thirst for firefighting knowledge was increasing. I would have a smattering of spiritual encounters in my twenty-five-year career. Yet it would take years before I would come to understand the impact they had on me.

. . .

I experienced my first structure fire at this station. Early one weekday morning, after just relieving the firefighter in the left jump seat, an alarm was transmitted for a house fire. I would respond with three firefighters from the previous shift. On arrival, I noticed a couple standing on the sidewalk leading into their concrete-block home. This house was set back quite a distance from the street. They were pointing to their home, to its left side, saying, "Fire is in the bedroom." From their open front door, I could see a light brownish gray smoke inside; this smoke was also outside hanging in the morning humid air.

Lieutenant John Hunt, who would later be appointed chief of the department, told his firefighter to pull one booster hose line, and I assisted. The firefighter went around to the left side of the house where the fire could be seen through the bedroom window. He took the front of the hardy nozzle and broke out a pane of glass in the casement window, opened the nozzle, and knocked down the fire. He then took the nozzle, with me behind him pulling the hose, back to the front door of the house and entered. I quickly put on my mask and followed. We went down the hall to the left and extinguished the small amount of fire that was still burning.

It all happened so quickly, and I was excited for the experience. I noticed Rescue 1 had arrived from Station 1, and the lone firefighter placed an electric smoke ejector fan in the open front door. I was told to open all the windows in the house. With the windows open and the smoke ejector fan hanging in the doorway the smoke dissipated quite rapidly. It wasn't long before the relief crews arrived in one of their personal cars and the firefighters from yesterday's shift piled into it and returned to the fire station.

This wasn't a roaring blaze with punishing heat, but it was my first structure fire, and I was definitely enthralled. It did produce some aftereffects that I'd come to recognize throughout my career, the main one being the distinct odor of a structure fire. This fire odor was different than the odor from a grass fire, leaves burning, or a campfire. This odor saturated my clothing, skin, and hair. I'd get whiffs of it throughout the rest of the shift, and when I took a shower that evening, the odor seemed to fill the stall as it exited the pours of my skin and rinsed from my hair. I also had a slight cough throughout the day. Even though I donned my mask before entering the structure, I still inhaled some smoke. I had never smoked cigarettes, but numerous firefighters did and may have had the ability to tolerate smoke better than I. The cough was gone by the next morning, but the odor hung around me for a few days, and I kept smelling it, especially when I washed my hair.

Experiencing this fire pushed me farther in my decision to request a transfer to Station 1. I talked it over with my lieutenant; he understood my desire and made the request for me. I believe without his support I may not have been granted the request. I would miss my conversations with Lieutenant Danny but knew a busier station was best for me and, I believe, for the department itself as well as the citizens of Orlando.

I reported to Firehouse 1 on a Friday. I was assigned to ride the tailboard of Engine 1. There were those times when an engine company had more than four crew members, so the additional firefighters rode standing on the tailboard and holding on to the parallel bar that ran just above the hose bed. If there was an extra firefighter on the tower ladder, they rode sitting on the cowling next to the turntable and facing forward toward the jump seat firefighter. They secured themselves by hooking their arm through the lowest ladder rung permanently mounted to the turntable.

With Saturdays being truck day, or apparatus day, Fridays were "station day." On this day, all firehouses would receive a more thorough cleaning. My cleaning assignment was to scrub the stair treads from the dormitory down to the first floor. I first used a small dust brush and metal dustpan to pick up the dirt. I then wet each individual step, sprinkled Comet on the tread, then scrubbed them with an 8-inch wooden bristle brush. Using a wet rag and warm water, I removed the dirty soap scum, leaving a nice clean step. This was one of the most undesirable assignments, but I thought nothing of it. I was just happy to be at Station 1, and I was accustomed to such tasks.

Since I was the newest firefighter on shift, I was assigned to ride different equipment. One day I would ride Engine 1, and on another day Engine 51 or the tower ladder. I even got to ride with engineer Bob Shawen on Rescue 1. Bob was known for his firefighting and rescue expertise. I was honored to ride with him, but because I was so new and inexperienced, I was concerned I may do something wrong or let him down. But I also realized I could learn a great deal about firefighting and rescue operations from him. In fact, there was another Engineer, Bob, assigned to Rescue 1 on another shift. Bob Cross and Bob Shawen were legendary in the department at that time.

I was on the emergency scene when Bob made a heroic rescue of a young man from a hotel balcony. Other crew members and I followed his guidance on the scene of a freight train versus pickup truck. The call came in one early afternoon. The location of the crash was where Colonial

Drive intersected with the railroad tracks. The way I understood the accident, the driver stopped his truck on the tracks, and, seeing the train coming, exited the truck and ran down the tracks. The train hit both the truck and the driver. When Engine 51 and Rescue 1 arrived on the scene, the locomotive of the train was a good 50 to 100 feet down the track. Witnesses said the man was under the locomotive.

As we got closer to the locomotive, just the size and sound of this massive machine was scary. I was apprehensive and wondered what could be done for this person. Bob never hesitated; he crawled under the small opening between the locomotive and train track. Due to such a confined space, all rescue personnel had to work on their stomachs with their backs up against the filthy and oily underside of the locomotive. The powerful engine was still running and made this rescue even more frightening. Under the expertise of Engineer Bob Shawen, we were able to extricate the victim. We loaded him into a waiting ambulance, and Bob, an EMT, road with the victim in the back of the ambulance to Florida Hospital. I'd drive Rescue 1 to the hospital to retrieve Bob. The middle-aged man did not survive due to his extensive injuries. Though this was tragic, I had been initiated into my new profession and its importance to the citizens of Orlando. I was also being mentored by the likes of Bob Shawen, and got to witness the conscientious efforts of the firefighters on Engine 51.

Bob also knew every street in the city and probably the county as well. When an alarm came in, he never hesitated to determine the best route. This was quite apparent one morning. I was assigned to ride with Engineer Shawen and around 9:00 in the morning we received a call to a shooting in the 600 block of east South Street. At that time an engine company wasn't assigned to respond to these calls.

I jumped in the passenger seat of Rescue 1 and out the door we flew. We took a left out of the station and a left on Anderson, a one-way street out of downtown. Making good time, with the light traffic at this time of day, we came to Summerlin Avenue, taking another left we passed underneath the East-West Expressway. Bob immediately turned right onto South Street, a one-way street leading into downtown, bucking the traffic. Bob knew, based on the street address, that the house would be either on the corner of Summerlin and South Street or a few houses down on the left. This was my first encounter "bucking" traffic. We were now responding the wrong way on a one-way street. It turned out the address was the second house on the left.

Bob's knowledge of streets and address numbers saved considerable response time and, during this call, possibly a life. Without his knowledge, we would have had to drive several more blocks to the next street that passed underneath the East-West Expressway. After turning left on to Mills Avenue, and then another left on to South Street, we would have to respond yet another five blocks to the scene. So it was definitely a good decision.

The rescue truck had stopped in front of the house, and an Orlando Police Department cruiser, responding on South Street, stopped in front of Rescue 1. Bob secured the first aid box and, not waiting on the police officer, headed through the front door. On the living room floor, we found a conscious man in his forties with six gunshot wounds throughout this body. A small caliber semiautomatic pistol was on the floor. Using the side of his foot, Bob slid the gun to the entering police officer, and we started to attend to the man's wounds, none of which were life threatening. The shooter, his teenage son, was crying. The father and his son were fortunate the gun wasn't a larger caliber. As we evaluated the victim, wrapping and covering wounds, he also started to cry. Both the son and father were extremely saddened for what just happened, and the father reassured his son that everything was going to be alright. From what I witnessed, I believe that father and son would solve what problems they were dealing with, and because of this incident, would grow closer in their love for one another. I left the scene with great compassion for them both.

• • •

I was definitely excited by my new profession, but I knew I had so much to learn. Though I was fortunate to be at Station 1 because there were numerous firefighters to learn from. One of those firefighters was Joe Samillano. He had been recently hired after spending a few years with the New York City Fire Department on Engine 45 in the South Bronx. As it turned out, we spent our careers working together on the same apparatus, rare at that time and probably unheard of today. Another member of the department was Assistant Chief Mike Kelly who also had a wealth of knowledge. There were others I would get to know, such as FDNY's Battalion Chief Pete Valenzano and Deputy Chief Vincent Dunn who had vast experience in structural fires and collapse of structures due to fire.

I also started reading *Fire Engineering* magazine. This publication came out monthly and a copy was provided for every firehouse. In 1976, *Firehouse* magazine was published, and I subscribed to it. I also signed up for fire-related classes taught by instructors from different fire departments in the local area, and some of those instructors were from out of town. One such instructor was an assistant chief with, I think, the Philadelphia Fire Department. He taught us the use of ropes and knots. He was very knowledgeable with good useful technique. He showed us how to throw a line to a third story window using only the rope. I found this ingenious but never had a situation where I would need to use it. He also taught us how to tie a knot known as the Spanish bowline. One use for this knot was to secure and raise or lower a stokes basket. Later this knot would come back to bite me, so to speak.

· · ·

I attended a two-day seminar taught by a well-respected retired captain from the New York City Fire Department. He had retired and became fire chief of a department in upstate New York. His well-received class was on forcible entry since he spent thirty years on a busy ladder company, thus gaining valuable knowledge. Towards the end of the class, he reflected on his thirty-plus years in the fire service. He made the comments that fire departments need to think about marketing themselves, especially those departments that aren't extremely busy emergency-wise. This seem to resonate with me; though our department was growing in emergencies, I understood his thoughts. He was basically saying fire departments need to get out into their communities and become more visible.

This was during the time of rapid growth of Disney World. Their growth spilled over to the city of Orlando. Family entertainment such as Rosie O'Grady's and the Cheyenne Saloon & Opera House became part of the Church Street Station. This downtown area had become a destination for family fun, especially on the weekends and evenings. Since our firehouse was centrally located a few blocks from this lively area we would drive our apparatus and park them on the streets. Folks from out of town had their pictures taken beside our shiny new apparatus with the Orlando Fire Department emblem in the background. I always carried a small inexpensive 35mm camera that hung from the turn signal handle. I would offer to take pictures of families or children for those who wanted their pictures taken but didn't have a camera. I would take the picture, not promising the quality, and send it to them. I was happy to do that, especially for a family on vacation.

Rosie O'Grady's and the fire department had a good relationship. The restaurant would provide meals at times to the two firehouses that responded to their establishments to show their appreciation for our professional services. We took the opportunity to get involved as much as possible when the Church Street Station complex asked us to participate in one of their street activities. One was to gather twelve fire departments from throughout the state to have a barbecue cooking competition at their complex. We were of course invited, and it was well received by the community. Our team was led by Firefighter Pat Hughes, an excellent cook with expertise in barbecue. The Cheyenne Saloon provided the beef and pork, and each team added their secret sauces and spices. Six teams were lined up on the street in front of Rosie O'Grady's, and six teams were directly across the street in front of the Cheyenne Saloon. After cooking all night, the aroma coming from the cookers blanketed the entire downtown area. Saturday was a cool spring day with blue skies. As folks began to enter to enjoy the day and competition, the "good time dancers" from the saloon spilled out into the street. One young lady grabbed a firefighter assigned to Rescue 1 to dance with her. She may or may not have known how well he could dance. They became a hit with all stopping to watch. What a wonderful day with good memories. All proceeds were donated to a charitable organization, so it was even more fun and rewarding.

We continued to stay involved in the community. We participated in a bed race one beautiful Friday afternoon. Church Street was closed to automobile traffic and only for four-wheel beds. Our entry was headed by Engineer-Paramedic Ray Taylor. The team must have four pushers and one person who road on the bed. Their theme was a hospital bed with the white sheets flowing down around its sides. Ray and his team dressed in white doctors' coats, surgical hats, stethoscopes around their necks. The patient was dressed in the usual hospital gown. It was fun to watch and once again the fire department was pictured racing down the street with coats and sheets flying in the wind.

We participated in stair climbs at the Sun Bank Tower and almost all of the 5- and 10-kilometer road races. At that time minitriathlons were popular at the University of Central Florida and at Sea World. We would enter teams and participate. We wore our fire department T-shirts for exposure. Our involvement in the community was gaining interest with other organizations. We were working on a Habitat for Humanity house, and I saw a group of individuals from a local law firm wearing their T-shirts as well.

Momma B's, a local sandwich shop, asked us for fire department T-shirts. Mr. and Mrs. Momma B's wanted their young ladies who made the sandwiches to wear different T-shirts of companies in the community. They looked sharp in the T-shirts, and it became a hit with local businesses. My favorite sub sandwich was the "sloppy salami," an overflowing amount of egg salad with slices of salami tucked between the egg salad and soft roll. The "sloppy" came in when you ate it. This sandwich was impossible to eat without making a mess; every bite forced egg salad to spill out, but it was worth the mess, so very tasty. We always took extra napkins when ordering them.

. . .

I also worked as many overtime days as I could, not so much for the extra income but more the experience. I was definitely enthusiastic. I trained and did my best to understand the equipment used for firefighting and rescue operations. One piece of equipment I would use and get to know quite personally was the Partner K1200 power saw. This gasoline-powered circular saw weighed around 30 pounds. The saw was used for numerous applications, such as ventilating roofs and cutting openings in roll-up doors—the saw was somewhat cumbersome if we had to cut in front or overhead. I knew I would have to start a workout routine to gain strength to handle this saw with proficiency and safely. I envisioned myself being comfortable enough to write my name in cursive in a roof.

One afternoon we were at the emergency room, but I don't remember the reason why. Sandi Fraser, the triage nurse that day, was also a neighbor, so I knew her well. Not only was she an exceptional proficient nurse but also hilarious and quick witted. Pinned to her scrubs was a small metal button that read I Want It All. I immediately thought of my profession. I too wanted it all. I wanted to experience all facets of the job. I wanted to be proficient and professional, and I was willing to put in the time and effort. I asked Sandi where she got the button and the next day I went and purchased one and affixed it to my fire helmet next to the shield. It's still there all these years later but barely legible due to heat, smoke, and soot.

. . .

On a weekday midmorning I was riding the tailboard of Engine 1. We, along with Engine 2, were dispatched to a house fire in their first response territory. I don't remember the name of the street; it ran between Beggs Avenue and North Terry Avenue. Since we were the second due engine company, we were told to bring in one 2½-inch supply line to Engine 2. We stopped at the fire hydrant at the intersection at Beggs Avenue. I could see black smoke coming from the small wood frame private dwelling down the street. I reached up into the hose bed, secured the 2½-inch hose and hydrant wrench and stepped to the street. I wrapped the hose around the hydrant, stepping on the hose with my left foot I told the driver to go. As the engine pulled away, hose hitting the street, I placed the hydrant wrench on the stem nut on top of the hydrant and quickly removed one of the two 2½-inch port caps by hand. Often these caps weren't so easily removed, and the hydrant wrench was needed for leverage. I screwed the hose coupling to the port and made sure the hose was laid in such a way it wouldn't kink when the hydrant was opened.

It seemed like only seconds when I heard three blasts from Engine 2's air horns, they were ready for water. Grabbing the hydrant wrench I quickly turned the five-sided stem nut counterclockwise allowing water to move from the water main, up through the hydrant and flow through the hose line to Engine 2. I then followed the hose line, straightening any kinks in the hose. I would then report to the engineer of Engine 2 to see if he needed any assistance. Saying no, I quickly followed the 1½-inch hose line to the front door.

Seeing the volume of this dense smoke and all that was happening, I definitely wanted to experience such a fire. So, at the front of the open doorway, I quickly donned my mask. Just inside the doorway were Firefighters Nick Graham and Dave Baldino. Apparently, Dave found an unconscious dog and handed it to Nick, who began mouth-to-mouth resuscitation and, seeing me on the porch, thrusted the puppy into my arms and said take him. I immediately took the dog, went to Rescue 1 and secured the E&J Resuscitator off the truck. Laying the small puppy on its side in the front yard I cupped the oxygen mask over the dog's nose. Not knowing what else to do, I massaged its small chest with my free hand while I held the mask over its snoot. Red Huber, an *Orlando Sentinel* photographer was on the scene and took a picture of me resuscitating the puppy named Toby. The next day Toby and I were pictured in the newspaper. Toby recovered, and I was the hero firefighter who rescued him. Red's photo went to Associated Press and was now in other newspapers throughout the country. I received thank you cards and letters, and money and a marriage proposal from a young lady in Ohio. I also received a nice steak dinner from LaCantina Steakhouse restaurant for my compassion for animals. Though I do have a love and compassion for animals, I felt uncomfortable with all the notoriety because I didn't make the rescue. I didn't even make it inside the house, but I guess I did help to save the life of Toby.

About this same time in my young career, I was assigned to ride Engine 1. Around 9:00 on a weekday morning we were dispatched with Engine 5 to a house fire on Florida Avenue. Arriving second due, I noticed no fire showing but light lazy smoke making its way out of every opened window and doorway. Seeing heat and air conditioning trucks on the scene indicated work was being done. It turned out new ductwork was being installed throughout the house. Apparently, a mastic used to join the sections of metal ductwork somehow caught fire inside of the duct. Engine 5 had stretched a booster hose through the front door. We were instructed to pull another booster from our apparatus to the back door.

I want to again add that we didn't have standard operating procedures at that time, also at that time ladder companies weren't assigned to respond to house fires, only building fires.

Since the booster nozzle facing the house was on my side the lieutenant told me to pull the booster line. Being in a hurry, I secured the nozzle before stepping down to the street level. As I did, the bottom of my turnout coat hooked over the top of the vertical handrail so when I made my final step down to the street I just hung there, feet dangling in the air. Flailing back and forth trying to get even one foot back to the step I heard my fire coat rip. Releasing my grip on the nozzle allowed me to use my hands to stabilize myself to get my feet back on the step. I'm sure this looked comical; I was embarrassed and frustrated.

The lieutenant was heading down the driveway next to the house. As I found my footing on the step, a firefighter ran to the truck, grabbed the nozzle lying on the ground, and took off toward the lieutenant. When he reached the lieutenant, I reached up and grabbed hold of the hose rolling off the reel to help with the stretch and for extra hose if needed. The firefighter with the nozzle stopped at an open window on the side of the house, where fire was coming from an open floor register just below the window. With the window being waist high he pointed the nozzle through and down toward the fire and open the nozzle. The fire appeared to go out but as soon as he released the handle to stop the flow of water the fire returned. Feeling I wasn't doing anything constructive, I felt I should find my lieutenant.

I went around to the back door of the house and saw the chief in command of the fire. He told me to search the house. I was more than willing and donned my air mask. Entering through the back door, I stayed low crawling on hands and knees. The hallway was maybe 3 feet wide, narrow enough to be easily searched and to make contact with both sidewalls. When I got to my first opening my visibility was now zero. I stayed left, keeping my left hand in contact with this wall and baseboard. I now made wide sweeps out into the room with my right hand and foot. I had a feeling I was in the kitchen. What was important was to keep contact with the wall on my left and do my best to remember when I made a turn into another room.

As I made my way down the wall I came to a doorway. I entered and again stayed on the left wall. I had now made two left turns. I felt I was in a pantry because of canned goods I encountered on low shelves. As I continued my left-handed search, I came to a fourth wall and felt I would come to the door I had entered. But for reasons I still don't understand I could not find my way out. This pantry only had an open floor space of approximately 6' x 6', but I was just circling the room, unable to find the doorway. I started getting concerned, as I had started breathing rapidly from my MSA (mine safety appliances) air pack and, with this added stress of not being able to find my way out, I was breathing even harder. The low air alarm bell started to ring, and I became even more anxious. Breathing became difficult, and I could feel the mask around my face pulling tighter on each forced breath. But suddenly, I found a closed door. I possibly had kicked it closed making the search. I found the doorknob and opened the door. I was having much difficulty getting any air from my air pack, inhaling with such force that I felt I could collapse the walls of the heavy steel air tank used at that time. I made a right hand turn out the doorway, heading back in the direction I came from. When I got to the next opening and made the right turn, I could see light coming from the open back door. I was now in the hallway moving quickly to get outside and remove my mask.

Once outside the back door I grabbed the bottom of the mask, just under my chin, and pulled out and up, ripping it off. In doing so my newly acquired leather fire helmet bounced across the grass. I was now safe, gulping in the cool fresh air.

Not considering what just happened I quickly returned to the truck to change out my empty air cylinder. With a full air cylinder on my back, I return through the front door and met up with Engine 5's crew. They had now found the origin of the fire and extinguished it as best they could. Engineer David Barker off of Rescue 1 brought in a K-1200 gasoline power saw and cut out the wooden flooring around the register, allowing Engine 5's crew to overhaul the fire.

From my point of view, my performance at this fire was terrible. The fire coat incident was embarrassing and getting disoriented in the pantry could have cost me my life. Though I did learn some valuable lessons at this fire that would help me in the future, I was still bummed.

I was also disappointed in our department. We lacked leadership, guidance, and cohesiveness. Some type of SOPs (standard operating procedures) and tactics would have been very helpful. We did put the fire out, but we did a lot of unnecessary damage to this old yet beautifully kept home.

I had now been on the job about three years and had found my niche so to speak. After riding and responding to emergencies on the different apparatuses, I had found the tower ladder was my best fit. Working alongside Firefighter Joe Samillano helped me understand the value of SOPs. Since Joe was quite familiar with FDNY's SOPs, he would explain how the different apparatuses would work together as a team: how on a structure fire the engine company would be stretching the hose lines, while the ladder company opened up the building, gaining access for the engine companies, and to start search and ventilation. The command chief would evaluate the structure and keep track of the location and progress of the companies. Since I had spent a couple of years in the military, I did have a concept and saw firsthand the importance of individual units contributing their expertise to the overall success of an operation.

. . .

Firefighter Joe brought his FDNY manuals to work for us to read and review. Firefighter Grant Aiello, whose father was a member of the Chicago Fire Department, threw out the idea that we should visit and ride with the FDNY. I was certainly in favor of this idea. Joe contacted his old Battalion Chief Pete Valenzano, and Pete made all the necessary arrangements. Pete would even pick us up at LaGuardia Airport at 1:00 a.m. and take us to the firehouse where we would stay.

Around two in the morning we pulled up to the quarters of Engine 46, Ladder 27, and Battalion 56 in the South Bronx. Since it was winter, we were greeted by below freezing temperatures. As we walked through a small doorway in front of the firehouse, I was immediately hit by the smell of structure fire that permeated the air. With my nose taking in this distinct aroma, my eyes focused on the tip of the 100-foot rear mount aerial. It was blackened and charred from ventilating windows. The house-watch firefighter was aware of our pending arrival. He had a firefighter who was in the kitchen show us our beds and a place to store our luggage.

We were treated extremely well. All shifts, or "tours" as they call them, would not allow us to pay for any meals. They would impress upon us that we were guests and that "guests don't pay," though we insisted that we help with dishes and station cleanup. This would be one of the many lessons we learned and would take back to our Orlando firehouse: a guest at our table will never pay for a meal.

One midmorning in New York City, we were shopping for the next meal on Arthur Avenue in Little Italy, when the lieutenant of Ladder 27 bought us a slice of pizza. I have never seen a slice of pizza this large. The lieutenant, seeing me fumble with the large wedge, showed me how to fold it for ease of eating. Shopping for the meal was interesting and quite an experience. I was used to shopping at Publix grocery store, where all items were purchased from this one store. In Little Italy, mom-and-pop businesses lined Arthur Avenue. For meat, there was a butcher shop, for fish there was a fish market where selected seafood was lined up on chopped ice-covered tables just outside the front door. The same went for bakery items and pastries. I must add that I had never had a cannoli, but the firefighters raved about how good they were. I don't remember the pastry shop we entered but before we left for home, I bought shells and filling to hand-carry home. On our numerous return trips to the Bronx, we'd always visit this same shop and load up with cannoli. On one return trip home, I had a bag of cannoli shells and a large container of filling resting on my lap. The flight attendant, seeing what I had and quite familiar with this pastry shop, smiled and said, "They're so good." I immediately asked if she would like one. "Well, sure," she said, and retrieved a butter knife from first class; I filled a few shells. She shared them with her coworkers. Upon landing she and her coworkers gave me a bottle of champagne for sharing the cannoli.

Another thing I enjoyed with the New York City Fire Department was the camaraderie. They were a close, tightly knit team, all for one and one for all. I had witnessed that type of camaraderie in Vietnam and saw how important it was for a successful operation. One evening in the kitchen, I talked with a senior firefighter who worked with Dennis Smith on Engine Company 82. Dennis wrote the book *Report from Engine Company 82*. He shared with me what it was like during the "war years" in the late 1960s and '70s. The BBC had made a documentary, *Man Alive: The Bronx Is Burning*, that focused their story on Engine 82, Ladder 31, and Battalion 27. He added that it was crazy during that period; they would put out a fire and immediately be dispatched to another. Battalion Chief Pete Valenzano, who also worked during that time, told me he was standing in the street in command of a large vacant tenement building with fire showing from every window and looking up the street to see two more buildings on fire. Clearly arson fires were still being fought, though thankfully not quite at the volume they were during the war years.

On one of our trips, I was talking to a firefighter just starting his evening tour on Ladder 27. He said he felt it was going to be a busy night because of it was a warm Friday in addition to the kids being out of school. He was correct. Around 7:00 p.m., the firefighter on house-watch came over the intercom saying, "Everyone goes." He then rang a bell. Two taps on the bell sent two rings throughout the firehouse for the engine company to respond—three taps on the bell are for the ladder company, four taps was for the chief. I heard them also say after sending out the bells: "Engine, truck, chief, get out," or "Everybody goes."

Responding just as it was getting dark the streets were filled with people and activity. Since I was riding in the front seat between the officer and driver of Ladder 27, I heard the first arriving company transmit a "10-75," indicating a fire. On our arrival the driver, or "chauffeur," positioned the 100-foot aerial ladder truck in front of the building. As I exited the truck it appeared there was a street party going on. Folks in lawn chairs were sitting in the street as if to watch a show or movie. Children were everywhere, climbing on the parked apparatus having a grand time. Fire was showing from a few second story windows but the windows and doors on the ground floor were boarded up with plywood and metal.

As more windows began to show fire the crowd would applaud or raise their voices in excitement. Engine 46 was hooking up to a hydrant, and Ladder 27 was raising their aerial ladder to the roof of this four-story building. Hand lines were being stretched as the ladder company was using their power saw to cut the plywood covering the entrance door. As more companies arrived the festivity increased. The chief in command knowing the danger of this vacant building had ordered all companies out of the building and off the roof.

Ladder 27's aerial was retracted and secured in its cradle, then moved so a tower ladder could take their position in front of the building. Two more tower ladders were special called; one was placed on the side of the building, while the other was also positioned in front of the building to use their heavy caliber bucket streams to extinguish this now fairly well-established fire. This made for more excitement, but most of the on-lookers knew it was only a matter of time until the fire was extinguished, and the fun was over.

As I stood and watched the fire, I also watched the people. I was told that most likely one of the locals set the fire for the entertainment and fun of it. As the tower ladders did their work, Ladder 27 was told to take up and return to service. A firefighter of the truck told me many of these folks will be born, live, and die in this five-block area. He wasn't being judgmental, just stating the facts at that time. There was such poverty and few opportunities to escape this jungle so to say.

We loaded up and started heading back to the firehouse. We pulled over in front of a small market to buy some cold drinks. As some of the crew members headed inside, I stood on the sidewalk next to the curb, looking at the chipped curb, crack sidewalk, and splattered stains of who knows what. I wondered what this small worn, abused patch of concrete had seen. I had also noticed the stone stair treads in tenement buildings were worn and cupped from years of occupancies ascending and descending. I pondered the history of those stairs, the smooth worn steps, chipped in places, paint splattered, with dirt and grime encased in the joints could never be reproduced, except through the years of their existence. To live and die in this old historic borough and never see another side of living outside of it is heartbreaking for me.

· · ·

I took the opportunity to ask questions and learn as much as I could about structural firefighting and FDNY operating procedures. I was fortunate to be able to witness and understand the importance of ventilating roofs and how the roof man and outside vent man operated. FDNY's standard operating procedures were quite expansive, and the department didn't lack for equipment and manpower. This wasn't the case with the Orlando Fire Department, not only did we not have SOPs, but we didn't have the resources like the FDNY.

One other thing I noticed was how simple and straight forward their apparatus was. It was designed for firefighting, with no bells and whistles. The firefighters' priorities centered around its operation and the tools in its compartments, rather than its appearance.

One morning around 11:00, we were dispatched to an H-type multiple-dwelling tenement fire. The H referred to the configuration of the building from above." We would be the second ladder company due to arrive.

Arriving on the scene I saw fire from one window, top floor, at a corner apartment. Firefighter Bowser was assigned the roof man position that day. Grabbing the power saw from its compartment, he said, "Follow me." Moving quickly, I followed him to the attached adjoining building, and we started up its interior staircase. With the saw slung over his shoulder, Bowser was taking every other stone step as he headed to the roof bulkhead. I didn't have on firefighting equipment, nor did I have a heavy saw, yet I had to move rapidly to keep up. Bowser knew the importance of getting to the roof—this was a top-floor fire and they had to keep the fire out of the cockloft (the space between the ceiling of the top-floor apartments and the roof system that kept rain and snow out of the building). As we passed through the unlocked roof bulkhead door he told me to wait at the parapet, the 2-foot-high wall that separated the two buildings. On that clear crisp day, I had an excellent vantage point to view the roof operation.

Once stepping over the parapet, Bowser removed the carrying sling, threw it aside, and pulled the starting rope a few times; the saw started. Since this was an inside corner of the H-shaped building, there was still a concern if the fire did get into the cockloft it could spread throughout the

entire cockloft and eventually make its way to the "throat" of the building, or the middle of the building, the perpendicular line that connects
the two parallel lines of the H. If the fire got to the throat and made its
way through to the other side now you've got both sides of the building's
cockloft on fire. With one saw already operating, Bowser would assist with
his saw, enlarging the ventilation opening. The additional firefighters had
6-foot Halligan hooks to remove the roofing material cut by these saws. It
seems like only minutes when I saw a spray of water exiting the front and
side windows of the fire apartment. As the engine company worked their
way deeper into the apartment the nozzle man whirled the straight-tip
nozzle, causing a spray of water to pop through the ventilation opening.
This engine company did what they do best: locate, confine, and extinguish the fire. With their aggressive knock down, the black smoke turned
to a whitish gray, a most welcoming sight to the chief in command.

The roof men then cut a few small triangular inspection holes to make
sure the fire hadn't entered the cockloft. I was fortunate to have witnessed
such a straightforward, smooth operation. Not all fires go that smoothly;
in fact, very few do, but when they do, it's very rewarding to the firefighters. I saw firsthand how SOPs made for such a successful operation. All
companies had a task to complete, and they each knew their assignment
was equally important to the overall success of this fire. We could see the
importance of SOPs and felt our department could benefit from them.

•   •   •

We continued to ask questions and visually learn. The lieutenant from
Ladder 27 took us across the street from the fire house to a vacant building and showed us the different ways of forcing doors using a Halligan
bar and a flat-headed axe. Orlando Fire Department's forcible entry tool
at that time was the hux bar. I personally didn't see its usefulness and was
never given instructions on how to use it. Just having the Halligan and
axe for forcing doors would be a great improvement, plus the Halligan
bar alone had many other uses as well. I liked how this 30-inch Pro-Bar
Halligan, made by K-Tool Manufacturing, could be married together
with the flat-headed axe for convenience of carrying. Our department
still carried the pick-headed axe that shouldn't be used to strike the end

of the Halligan tool. Also, our department's flat-headed axes were fairly lightweight; a heavier axe would work much better.

Another tool we felt would be useful for pulling down ceiling was the Halligan hook. Our department used the traditional pike pole to perform this task. The pike pole has its place in the arsenal of firefighting tools, but I could see the advantages of the Halligan hook. The Z-shaped head of this hook was wider so after it was thrust through a ceiling, whether it was lath and plaster or drywall; it would grab a larger area bringing down a larger section, exposing the area more quickly.

Our first trip was filled with activities. We didn't just witness some good-working fires but visiting the training academy, a fireboat, and different firehouses. One such firehouse was Engine 82 and Ladder 31. This was the firehouse centered around Dennis Smith's book, *Report from Engine Company 82*." All firefighters we met were cordial and willing to share their knowledge. These were very busy companies with experience firefighters. A probationary firefighter could learn a great deal working in the South Bronx. One such firefighter I met was John Jay Jonas, assigned to Engine Company 46. He was a quiet young man. I watched as he diligently went over the apparatus every morning at the start of his shift. I could see how serious he took the job. He was definitely getting his share of experience. One firefighter lightheartedly remarked that "every time Jonas works, we go to a fire." John had a very successful career with the FDNY as captain of Ladder 6, who survived the collapse of the twin towers. Numerous articles and videos had been made about him, his crew, and the rescue of Josephine Harris.

As our trip came to an end, I was filled with hope for the future of the Orlando Fire Department. I don't remember who took us to Kennedy International Airport that cold clear afternoon. After checking our bags, we noticed a haze of smoke filling the terminal. It wasn't long before we were told to evacuate the building. We saw in the distance the apparatus of the FDNY arriving on the scene. I don't remember the cause of the fire, but we made our flight after standing outside for so long I became quite cold. Grant was kind to give me his jacket; he's just that sort of person.

The return home flight was quiet with some seats unoccupied. Joe and I sat next to each other at the front of the plane. As evening approached, we began to talk about our trip. Joe made the comment that maybe we could put together some form of SOPs using the FDNY's as a guide. On the quiet flight back to Orlando, we sat and talked about how this could possibly be done.

Our next shift back to work, we approached our Assistant Chief Mike Kelly and pitched Joe's idea. Chief Kelly started the wheels turning. A committee of firefighters were assembled to review the ideas brought back from our trip. It took about a year to come up with a basic operating procedure. Once it was approved by Gene Reynolds, the chief of the department, it would be presented to the troops.

I was asked to present our first ever SOPs to the entire department. To this day I don't know the reason I was asked. It may have been because I had recently started teaching classes at the academy. But the classes I taught were considered hands-on classes, such as ladders and forcible entry. These were subjects I knew fairly well and was comfortable demonstrating their use. But I had never made a presentation in front of a formal classroom setting. I did feel honored to be asked, and I did know the concept and the subject quite well, but I also knew my verbal communication abilities were lacking. I just wasn't sure I was the person for this very important change of policy. Now that I look back on it, this should have been presented by a higher-ranking individual. I now think the chief of training, or the deputy chief of combat, should have been selected.

The day came for my first ever presentation, from 9:00 to 12:00, followed by another class I had to teach in the afternoon. Different companies throughout the city were taken out of service to attend. I felt this three-hour block of time would be adequate, but I was informed at the start of class that the chief of training had decided to use some of this time to present and discuss an issue not relating to the SOPs. I don't remember what he spoke about, as my mind was focused on my presentation, with my handwritten notes stacked neatly on the table in front of me. With this added presentation I was concerned I may not have enough time for the SOPs. It turned out the chief's presentation lasted two hours; this left me less than an hour for the SOPs. I was now nervous and stressed, as I knew I didn't have the time to adequately present this important and controversial subject. I wish then that I had respectfully declined to present at this time due to the limited time.

I was now even more nervous, and I believe it showed, but decided to present anyway. I quickly started to explain these new procedures yet knew I just didn't have enough time. I also knew I was doing a poor job, and I'm sure the firefighters sitting before me were having a difficult time understanding what I was trying to explain. It wasn't long before I received pushback and criticism. They had some valid points that the committee hadn't considered or even thought about. One reaction that I wasn't expecting was the number of firefighters not in favor of having SOPs. I couldn't understand this. I knew this would make for more accountability for the company officer and some firefighters, but it would greatly improve our tactics, plus provide a safer emergency scene for all.

There were those firefighters who questioned why we were using FDNY's SOPs as a model for ours. Why not Atlanta's? Or Phoenix's? They had a point, but we felt the FDNY had good solid SOPs that had been tried and tested.

I was still encouraged that our department was moving in the right direction. But after my failed presentation, and pushback from some firefighters, the date to implement our first SOPs would have to be rescheduled. There were some details that had to be worked out involving the departments senior managers.

As for me personally, I was embarrassed by my performance. One lieutenant that had attended the class was quite critical of me. I was hurt and felt bad, but I could understand his criticism. I was in over my head. I had never worked with this particular lieutenant but respected him and considered him a good officer. His criticism was humbling and as much as we human beings don't like to be criticized, in this instance, it was deserved. All these years later, it's easy to see how important this SOP presentation was, and to have me be the one to present such important information to my fellow firefighters was a disservice to them.

One other problem we had at that time was getting the equipment needed to implement the SOPs. One example was the SOPs had stipulated that the ladder company's forcible entryman was to carry a 30-inch Halligan bar and flat-headed axe. There were different manufacturers for these bars, but we had requested the 30-inch Pro-Bar, made by K-Tool Manufacturing. This was the exact same bar the FDNY used, and after the bar was evaluated, we could see why. The forks were longer and wider with a slight concave curve so it would slip easier between the door and its jamb. The adz end also had a similar curve to it and the pick was slim, making it better for padlocks. The 30-inch length made it perfect to marry together with the flat-headed axe. But the bars we received weren't the Pro-Bar; they lacked in quality, and there wasn't one 30-inch bar in the order. The shortest was 36 inches and a few were 42 inches. If trying to force a door at the end of a narrow hallway the 36-inch may possibly be too long, and the 42-inch would definitely be too long. It took a while, but they were finally replaced with the 30-inch Pro-Bar.

. . .

I don't remember how long the SOPs were sidelined. There was still some grumbling and pushback, but I knew in time SOPs for operating on the scene of most structural fires would be adopted. And they were. Like any procedures, however, changes may need to be made to them for reasons such as safety or new technology. In my twenty-five-year block of time with the fire department, I witnessed successful operations specifically due to these SOPs.

Not long after the SOPs were instituted, I worked a fire that could have turned out differently if we hadn't adopted them. One cool February afternoon I was returning home from the Western Auto store at the corner of east Colonial Drive and Shine Street. Since this store was fairly close to my house, I always enjoyed taking residential brick streets. I noticed an older woman moving quickly across her front yard toward the street. I immediately saw her concern; smoke was showing from the top of two windows on her front porch and one side window just off the porch. I pulled my car into the driveway across the street and ran to her. She stated her husband, Jim, was still inside. I quickly ran to the screen door on the front porch. Just in that short amount of time, sporadic tongues of fire were now showing from the tops of the windows. Dropping to my hands and knees, I noticed through the screen door that the wooden jalousie window door was standing open to my right. Pulling open the screen door I was hit with dense smoke. I lowered my head, took a deep breath, and entered. I immediately dropped to my stomach as I heard the sound of electrical arcing coming from somewhere over the doorway. As sparks began to rain down, I made a bad decision. Instead of staying in contact with an interior wall I moved straight forward, deeper into the structure trying to get away from the frightening sound of wires arcing. In my prone position, I could see only inches in front of me. With my face to the hardwood flooring, I gasped for breath. With each rapid exhalation I saw dust moving across the floor. With difficulty breathing, I had a decision to make. Looking to my right was blackness and the distinct orange glow of burning gases at the ceiling. I also felt the radiating heat. Turning my head left I could see a brightness, sunlight making its way through the windows. Do I go right, deeper into the fire, or bail out to the left? The decision was made for me. As I continued to call for Jim, I heard a muffled moan coming from my right. I immediately started to craw that way, calling Jim's name.

I quickly went from hardwood flooring to carpet and felt I may be in the living room. The heat wasn't too bad, maybe because it was venting out the front windows. I could hear, from my right, the crackle of the fire and glass breaking from the heat. Moving blindly, I continued to crawl deeper into the room. Then, all of a sudden, I found him. He was unconscious, lying on his back, with his head toward the rear of the house. I was fortunate to find him in this position. My instinct was to drag Jim away from the fire.

Rolling Jim to his left side, his back now toward me. I wrapped my right arm under his right arm and around his chest. My right upper arm and shoulder were in his armpit. I reached my right hand under his left arm and torso. Luckily Jim wasn't an overly large man, and I was relieved when I was able to move him a few inches at a time. It was exhausting sliding Jim on the thick carpet. I was breathing hard but making progress. Using my legs and left arm I continued to slide Jim toward the rear of the house. I could now hear in the distance the sound of the siren and air horn coming from Engine Company 4. I continued to drag Jim, and when the carpet turned to linoleum, I felt I was in another room, possibly the kitchen. The smooth linoleum made it easier to slide Jim.

When I heard Engine 4's air brake engage, I knew they had arrived. I could also hear the sirens of the rest of the first alarm assignment making their way to the scene. Continuing to slide Jim, I came to a wall. Looking down the wall I saw light coming from a window. I dragged Jim up to this window. After taking in a breath of air at floor level, I reached up to try unlocking the window to open it but was unsuccessful; it may have been jammed or painted shut. I noticed the telephone table next to the window. I pushed the heavy black rotary telephone to the floor, took in another breath at the floor, grabbed the table with both hands, and smashed it into the window. The table shattered, breaking only a few panes of glass of this substantial double-hung check rail wooden window. Seeing the telephone on the floor, I replaced the headset back on its base. Wrapping my right hand around the headset and base I took another breath at floor level. Raising up I smashed the bottom of the base into the window, which was, thankfully, successful. I continued to break the window even more and the noise alerted the neighbors who called for the firefighters on Engine 4. Firefighter Tim Kingsbury came to the outside of the window and broke out the rest of the glass. I stuck my head out and got a few breaths of fresh air, then reached down to lift Jim to the window. Rolling Jim back to his stomach I lifted his upper torso to the windowsill, Tim and the neighbors were able to pull him through as I guided his legs.

Rescue 6 was now on the scene and started treatment. When an ambulance arrived, they helped load Jim and he was transported to Florida Hospital South. Jim spent a few days in the hospital due to smoke inhalation, and we both received minor lacerations from glass shards when I helped pass him through the window. I faired much better than Jim, most likely because of our ages and because Jim was in the structure longer.

As I made my way around to the front of the house, Engine 4's crew had advanced a 1¾-inch hose line through the front door and was extinguishing the fire. By now, all first-alarm companies had arrived. They had made a thorough search of the entire structure and were now overhauling the fire.

I had finally experienced what it might be like for a citizen of Orlando to have a fire in their home. I hoped they'd felt the Orlando

Fire Department was professional and experienced, having the necessary training and expertise to rescue them and extinguish their fire if in the same situation.

Experiencing this fire also showed me the value of SOPs. If I had become unconscious, I felt confident the firefighters would have rescued us in time to save our lives.

I don't know the amount of time I was inside the structure—perhaps five to ten minutes. I remember the difficulty with breathing from the moment I entered and wondered how I was able to accomplish the task without being overcome by the smoke. I would like to believe I had some help.

. . .

Not only seeing the importance of the FDNY's tactical procedures we longed to have the same camaraderie they had. We tried to encourage everyone to eat meals together. We started a syndicate where everyone contributed a small amount to have coffee, sugar, spices and the newspaper delivered. We also collected the same amount for the cost of the meal wether it was hot dogs or steak. At that time, it was $5.00, if we had money left over it went to the syndicate. When the funds became fairly large, we bought tickets to a basketball or hockey game.

Since our firehouse was quite large and well-staffed, a fellow firefighter, Bob Muenzner, built two 4 x 8-foot dining tables. Placing them end to end we now had plenty of room for firefighters and guests. Someone came up with the name Big House, and it became the firehouse's motto.

I loved the constant activity. We were fortunate to be chosen to evaluate new tools or techniques. By now, the administrative people, such as the chief of the department, his deputy chiefs, fire prevention, and arson investigation were moved to the newly built city hall building. We would no longer be referred to as "headquarters." We were Firehouse 1 and felt we had a home rather than being a showcase.

. . .

As Disney World grew, the city of Orlando grew in size and density. Fires and unusual emergencies were increasing. At our firehouse we needed to upgrade our procedures for water rescue. With the vast number of lakes and retention ponds, this upgrade was badly needed. Rick Stilp and Dewey Speegle, both engineer-paramedics, were sent to Fort Collins, Colorado, for extensive water rescue training. When they returned, they were instrumental in pulling together a proficient and professional team. New equipment was purchased, guidelines were written, and procedures were adopted.

Up to that point, when a call was received for a water rescue, the dispatchers would announce over the PA system, "Get the boat." This alerted all firefighters to move to the apparatus floor and hook the rescue boat to the trailer hitch on Rescue 1. Once hooked up and lights connected a lone firefighter, knowing how to scuba dive, would climb into the back of this small panel truck and change into a swimsuit. This could be quite difficult and hazardous because of being thrown from side to side during the response, plus the unsecured rescue tools were under their feet. When on the scene and the diver was needed to search for a victim there were no procedures. We would connect with any witnesses and do our best to identify the last known location, then begin our search. We only had a short period of time to find and revive them.

When I was a young boy, I swam often in lakes—Ivanhoe, Formosa, Rowena, Estelle, and Sue. At that time, they were quite clear; even without a mask I could easily see 8 feet or more. I remember their white sandy bottoms (it's sad they're no longer that way).

Upon Rick and Dewey's return, the city bought a new step van. Firefighter Roger Herota designed a sharp looking dive rescue logo and Firefighter Greg Muenzner painted Roger's design on each side of the truck. Rick, Dewey, and Bill Flakes, another firefighter, designed and built a well-thought-out vehicle, designed so the primary and secondary divers had adequate room to change into their wetsuits. The scuba tanks were mounted in the same way as the PBAs on the apparatus. All equipment was accessible and secure. It also had a large roll-up door at the rear of the truck, which provided openness and accessibility, and allowed natural light to enter. The only disadvantage was that it didn't have air conditioning. Trying to don a one-piece, fitted wetsuit in the middle of summer with high humidity was very difficult, especially if the response was only a few blocks away—though I'm not sure air-conditioning would have been much help. I'm glad I was young and agile. Rescue Boat 1 was finally in service. The city also purchased a new lightweight Zodiac boat to replace the heavy 16-foot fiberglass boat we had been using, but it had not yet arrived at this time.

But even the best plans or SOPs won't work if they're not followed. The dive team was still in its infancy, yet most firefighters at our firehouse knew the procedures and understood their importance. Sometimes it takes time for procedures to be fully excepted and followed, especially when they are new.

The district chief that day may have not fully understood the guidelines written for the response of the dive team. So, in his defense, the decision he made that day when the communications dispatcher said to "get the boat" may have influenced the decision he was about to make.

One other factor that may have influenced his decision was the new dive van had been taken out of service and sent to the fire department garage for preventive maintenance. The essential equipment for water rescue was taken off the dive van and placed in the back of our new heavy rescue truck. We would revert to our old way of responding and that was to wheel the boat to the back of Rescue 1 and secure it to its hitch.

Shortly after the announcement to get the boat, tones were sent out to Firehouse 1 and two. Equipment dispatched was Engine 2, Rescue 2, Rescue Boat 1, and the Command Chief. The location of the water rescue was at Rock Lake on North Orange Blossom Trail. The dispatcher confirmed a man was holding onto an overturned boat, and she directed all responding units to switch their radios to a different tactical frequency.

This day I was designated primary diver, John Williams, a firefighter-paramedic from Rescue 1, was assigned secondary diver. I immediately went and opened the two rear doors of the rescue and climbed in to change into my wetsuit. With my wetsuit half on, I noticed no activity at the rear of the truck. Why wasn't the boat being hooked up? Looking left out the rear doors I saw only the rear of the rescue boat leaving the station. Stepping down one step, I was able to see the chief's red suburban with the boat turning right onto Magnolia Avenue, its red lights flashing and electronic siren wailing.

About this time, John came up to me and told me what happened. The chief decided he and a driver would take only the boat, feeling it was only a boat retrieval. I knew it might turn out to be a bad decision, yet it never dawned on me to secure my dive bag and move it to the tower ladder. Within minutes the station alarm rang again, this time for Rescue 1. They and Engine 5 were dispatched to a cardiac in Engine 5's territory. I walked to the tower ladder and retrieved my portable radio so I could listen to the water rescue response.

The first unit to arrive was Rescue 2. From their vantage point on West Robinson Street, they gave the report of a man holding onto the side of an overturned boat, about 100 yards offshore. Within seconds, Rescue 2 reported the man was no longer visible. Hearing this, the commander, on the scene, requested the dive team be dispatched. The communications section, always professional and quick thinking, referred to the duty rosters given to them daily. Seeing I was the primary diver that day they would dispatch Tower Ladder 1 to the scene. One major problem: our dive equipment was on Rescue 1, and they were on the cardiac call. Luckily Rescue 1's call wasn't serious, and they were able to leave the patient in good hands with Engine 5's crew and the paramedics of the ambulance. Rescue 1 would respond, but they were quite a distance from Rock Lake.

The commander decided not to take the heavy fiberglass boat to the boat launch on the west side of the lake and got stuck in the soft beach sand behind the Parliament House Hotel. Though that spot was the closest access to the overturned boat, we were advised to respond to the rear parking lot of the hotel to assist with launching the boat.

Upon our arrival the overturned boat was about 75 yards from our location. I felt if I had on my wetsuit, swim fins, mask, and snorkel, I could possibly swim the distance to the boat, but to free dive with the buoyant wetsuit would be difficult.

Rescue 1 arrived with the dive gear, and, with the help of Engine 2's crew, we manhandled the boat off the trailer and launched it from the beach. We searched the general area until midnight. If I recall correctly, tomorrow's shift would search that entire day and on the third day his body would be recovered.

I've often wondered if it would have turned out differently if we'd have followed our SOPs. Could we have possibly gotten to this man in time to save his life?

. . .

One other water rescue call was quite bothersome for me. The call came in just at dusk at the south side of Lake Underhill. The report came in that a speed boat had hit a fishing boat. It was the middle of summer, so Lake Underhill was busy with speedboats, ski boats, and small jet skis. Not too many fishing boats used it because of the constant activity and wakes made by the recreational boaters. Most fishermen used the north side of the lake, which was separated by the East-West Expressway bridge into two large bodies of water. Apparently, a small fishing boat with a Vietnamese father and two small children was fishing fairly close to its south shoreline when a speedboat, not paying attention, ran over them.

Our response was quick in our new dive rescue truck with the light Zodiac boat hitched to it. I was the primary diver this day and had adequate time to don my wetsuit, secure my scuba tank, and pull my mask and snorkel down around my neck. I don't remember who the secondary diver was. When we got to the bridge over the lake, Lieutenant Samillano could see activity on the south side of the lake. We exited to our right at the Conway Road exit and took another immediate right onto Lake Underhill Road. Pulling off the roadway onto the grassy shoreline and coming to a stop I secured my swim fins in one hand and a rope bag in the other. Exiting the rear roll up door I headed the few feet to the shoreline. I overheard Assistant Chief Ray Hurn request Rescue 1 to respond; its large quartz lights would light up the scene. Out of my peripheral vision I saw a wet Vietnamese man and small boy at the water's edge. I'd also heard his daughter was missing. As I waded out into the water looking for any evidence or guidance from witnesses, I saw to my left a man pushing hard through the water; in his arms was a small unconscious child. I tossed my fins and rope bag to the shoreline and placed my arms under his to accept the small child. I immediately started mouth-to-mouth resuscitation and took her over to a waiting ambulance. After handing her to an ambulance attendant, I took off my scuba tank, and Lieutenant/

Paramedic John McCormack and I entered the side door. Continuing to do mouth-to-mouth, I looked out the side door into the concerned face of Jim Reynolds as he shut the door. John did his best to intubate the child, but it was too challenging in the vehicle as they were tossed side to side as the driver safely but frantically proceeded to the hospital. When arriving at Orlando General Hospital, I scooped her up, continuing mouth-to-mouth, and rushed her into the emergency room. I was disappointed in the reception, as no one responded to our emergency. In their defense, they may not have known we were responding to their location with a drowning victim. I laid the young child on a stainless-steel table and continued resuscitation. It seemed it took a while for hospital staff to come to our location. As a few personnel gathered I continued resuscitation and in time they took over.

I left and searched out a restroom to wash up. I stared into the wall mirror. My lower face was covered with partially wet and dried vomit aspirated from the young child. As I washed up, I was deeply moved and sorrowful by what happened. I so wanted this small Vietnamese child to survive. I had seen countless children her same age in Vietnam and felt if she survived, I would be giving back in some way to a cultural society I helped to destroy. This would not be the case; I was told she did not survive. I didn't ask any questions; I simply walked back to the room where I had left her and looked at her small frame lying peacefully on the table. Her shiny straight black hair was still wet.

I often wondered if we would have responded to Orlando Regional Medical Center, a level one trauma center, if she would have survived. It would have been one mile closer but also a few minutes longer.

. . .

As I look back over my fire department career, responding to dive calls were as challenging as any other emergency, but when those calls came in the nighttime hours, the stress and uncertainty was greatly increased. Perhaps it was due to the nights I spent in Vietnam. Light and visibility makes us feel safer and more secure.

One morning at 2:00 a.m., we responded to a report of a woman jumping from the bridge on the East-West Expressway where it crossed over Lake Underhill. Our response from the firehouse would quickly put us on the expressway and, within minutes, we would be on the bridge that crossed over this large lake. Empty of vehicles, we stopped on the bridge and asked communications if they had received any further information or was in contact with the caller. They advised us they had no further information but would call the caller back. Suspecting this was a bogus call, we drove to the boat launch area and met with the crews of Engine 11, Rescue 11, and the command chief.

Engine 11's crew assisted us in launching the boat and we motored over to the bridge. Communications responded back to advise us the caller was driving and saw a woman standing at the railing. The chief advised us via portable radio to put a diver in the water. I was the primary diver, so over the side I went. We had fairly adequate lighting due to the number of overhead lights illuminating the bridge. Lieutenant Samillano gave me one end of the search rope, and I looped it around my right wrist. Jim Reynolds, the secondary diver, sat on the boat's inflatable side, ready if needed. With my mask on and breathing through the scuba tanks regulator, I began to release air from my BC (buoyancy compensator).

Upon my descent, it was as if a light switch had been turned off. I had been in this situation before and knew what to expect, but I also knew I would never become comfortable. The longer it takes to come in contact with the bottom, never knowing what you may encounter when you reach it, is just plain scary, especially at night. I believe Orlando's local lakes were an average of only 13 feet deep; it wasn't the depth, however, but the zero visibility, along with not knowing what you might encounter. On that night, I encounter twisted steel rebar and large slabs of concrete resting at different angles. My only communication with the surface was the rope in my right hand. If I got in a situation where I needed help, I was to tug on the rope numerous times to alert the tender I needed assistance and to send a diver. This is when Jim would immediately respond by following my rope down to my location. That's why you always kept a firm grip on the end of the rope. With no visibility and no verbal communication, how else do you convey your emergency to your rescue diver?

Tonight, this dubious and dangerous search would last but a few minutes. It was decided that the information provided by this one caller wasn't reliable enough to continue the search and risk the safety of the dive team.

After loading the boat, we headed back to quarters. We would spend a couple of hours cleaning the boat and all equipment used. If not cleaned and dried, the lake water and slime could damage the scuba equipment that we depend on. All wetsuits, masks, fins, even the tending ropes if not cleaned in soapy water and hung to adequately dry, could produce an unpleasant odor and the growth of mildew. If we had gone through numerous air tanks, we would go to Firehouse 2 and refill them.

. . .

We responded one Saturday afternoon after a heavy thunderstorm to Lake Fairview, a fairly long response time from our quarters. The report was that a woman had been bitten by an alligator and was still in the water. The location was off the shoreline next to the train tracks running parallel to Orange Blossom Trail. Why would anyone want to swim in that area? That side of the lake had heavy undergrowth along its shoreline, a perfect place for alligators and water moccasins to live and nest. Luckily, she had made it to shore, and we were canceled before arriving but Engine 9's crew reported she had been bitten on her right leg.

Alligator sightings in Orlando's local lakes were becoming more frequent. Some became aggressive, and numerous dogs and cats had gone missing. It became a concern for the well-being of local lake residents, so the Florida Fish and Game Commission were dispatched to trap and remove them.

One morning when arriving to work I was told we would continue a search for a woman who had drowned the day before. The drowning was at the west side of Lake Ivanhoe, in College Park. Apparently, a woman went swimming and possibly an alligator attacked her. I had personally seen a large alligator in this lake around the peninsula of dense vegetation that was located in close proximity to where this woman was last seen.

The previous afternoon, C shift had worked for numerous hours to locate her from shore. If I remember the incident correctly, this woman arrived at the lake in her wheelchair, but was able to get to the water, leaving the chair by the shoreline. The wheelchair, along with a witness put her in this location.

A professional alligator hunter arrived on the scene and using his electric motor to patrol back and forth between the area of the last known sighting and the peninsula. He dangled raw meat attached to large fishhooks from his boat.

Working from the shore, per SOPs, the diver entered the water, holding one end of a rescue rope. The tethered line was then held by a firefighter at the shoreline, allowing the diver to make underwater passes back and forth in an arc, and covering an area that would resemble the shape of a section cut from a pie. The tender established two fixed points on the opposite shoreline. These two points determined the search area. When the diver reached one of those points, the tender then stopped the diver by giving two tugs on his end of the rope. The diver stopped, but before turning 180 degrees to swim back to the other fixed point, he wanted to extend his search about 6 feet. The tender, keeping tension on his end of the rope, slowly let out about 6 feet of rope. The diver swam away from the tension they're receiving; when they reached about 6 feet, the tender stopped them and the diver started their sweep back in the opposite direction. This shoreline operation, if I remember correctly, worked well up to about 100 feet, but this depended on a few factors: the bottom of the body of water; any holes or drop offs; and potential submerged obstacles, such as tree limbs and discarded objects, like shopping carts and bicycles that could snag the rope and impede the sweep of the diver. Beyond the 100 feet distance from the shoreline, we could now begin to work from the rescue boat.

The previous day's shift had searched into the night the maximum distance from the shoreline. On this day, we began our search from the boat approximately 75 feet from the shore. We first set two anchors, one off the bow and one off the stern, to keep the boat stable and in a fixed position. If the boat hadn't been anchored, the diver could easily pull the lightweight boat in the direction they were swimming. The anchored boat also offered a stable place or platform to control the divers search patterns. Firefighter Grant was assigned primary diver that day, and he entered the water. After reaching the bottom, he started a right-handed sweep. Dewey, Grant's line tender, was having Grant make his third sweep when Grant tugged three times on the rope, communicating to Dewey he had found the woman. Grant then tied the rope attached to a bright yellow pelican buoy to the body. Releasing the buoy, it rose to the surface and floated. If the diver had not done this and had instead left the body unsecured, it would have been difficult to find again due to zero-visibility. Grant did as he should have and made a sweep around the body to look for any suspicious items or evidence that might have involved the victim.

When Grant returned to the surface and was helped into the boat, Dewey and I entered the water. We followed the rope attached to the pelican buoy down to the victim and secured her inside a body bag. It used to be that we would bring the body to the surface, drag them to the shoreline or into the boat. It was not a very dignified way to treat a deceased person, and the news media was usually on the scene with cameras. Our new dive team SOPs were to place the victim inside a body bag for just such dignity. This happened to be our first attempt at this new procedure. After coming into contact with the victim, however, we quickly determined this wasn't going to work. For one thing, with the zero visibility, it was difficult to open the bag, and then maneuver the victim into the bag. Also, she was in the state of rigor mortis, and our bag wasn't large enough to accept an adult victim in this condition. We decided to bring her to the surface and secure her to the side of the boat and slowly motor to the shoreline where we then passed her to waiting Orlando police officers. We didn't notice any marks on her body that would indicate an alligator attack.

The revised water rescue procedures, equipment, and training greatly improved the department's professionalism in this area. The rapid and aggressive rescue attempt by C-shift personnel and the body recovery operation the next day went fairly well, but that didn't make up for the loss of life, and that's always a tragedy.

. . .

On another night, what should have been a routine dive call about scared the life out of me. The alarm was transmitted around 10:00 on a Saturday night for a car in a lake. The address was on West Ivanhoe Boulevard. On arrival Engine Company 3, Lieutenant Ray Masterson advised us of the situation. Apparently, a high school student had left their car running at the top of a steep driveway. Exiting the car to enter the house they must not have fully engaged the emergency brake causing the car to roll backwards down the driveway, across the brick street, over the curb, and down the bank into the lake. The car floated a fair distance out into the lake before it sank. We could see air bubbles raising from the submerged automobile.

We were to locate the automobile and check for any occupants. There was no presumed foul play, so we assumed it would be a simple automobile recovery. I was the primary diver this night with Jay Griner assigned as backup.

Jay Griner was another well-rounded firefighter. He was not only a member of the Dive Rescue Team, but also the High Angle Rope Rescue and the Hazardous Materials Team. He became a paramedic and, when he was appointed to the rank of lieutenant, would command Tower Ladder 1. Jay could weld, build, wire your barn, rope cattle, and shoe your horse. I don't think there wasn't anything he couldn't do.

A wrecker was being requested as I handed my rope bag to Jay, as he would be my line tender. I swam toward the location of the bubbles rising from the car. Just short of the bubbles, I deflated my BC, and down I went into the pitch-black water. When I contacted the bottom, I swam toward the car in the opposite direction from the tension Jay kept on the rope. As I got closer to the automobile, I saw a faint light, one of the taillights of the car. The car had rotated 180 degrees when it sank, this wasn't unusual nor that the lights were still illuminating. (I was once guided to a submerged automobile by the heat given off by the engine, though it was in the winter when the water temperature was lower).

As I got closer to the car, the taillight got brighter. When I placed my hand on the trunk the car alarm went off. My heart about burst from my chest. I had no idea a car alarm could sound beneath the water, but it did, and it scared me to death. Once I regained my composure and my heart was back in my chest, I moved to the left side of the car. I then tied the end of the rope to the back door handle. This confirmed that I had found the vehicle as well as its location. My next action was to search the car for any occupants. Since the windows were down in this small four-door compact car, I was able to extend my arms through them to search the small interior. Once I did this primary search, I slowly inflated my BC to return to the surface.

Returning to shore, I informed the incident commander of what I found. By now a wrecker was on the scene and had backed his truck up against the curb, just behind where Jay was standing. I then took the wrecker's J-hook with a short chain attached and followed the rope back to the vehicle. I was fortunate that the vehicle hadn't settled into the muddy bottom of the lake. I had to simply reach under the rear of the car and hook the J-hook to a substantial part on the frame or axle area. Keeping tension on the hook, I pulled the chain from under the vehicle so it laid straight and I could find it again. I then returned to the shoreline securing the wreckers winch cable and swam it back to the car. After hooking the cable to the chain, I kept tension on the connection so it wouldn't slip off and worked my way to the shore.

Still keeping tension, the wrecker driver started reeling in the cable. When the cable was taut, I moved away for safety. The wrecker slowly pulled the car from the lake. It would then be searched again and, if the vehicle had a trunk, it would also be opened and searched. Tonight, this was a fairly straightforward operation, except for the car alarm that probably took years off my life.

· · ·

The department was sometimes called upon for unusual types of rescues, such as baby ducks from a storm drain, raccoons from an attic soffit, cats and birds from trees, even snakes from inside of homes. These types of incidents were considered nonemergency, and if the unit was needed for an emergency call, they would be diverted.

When it came to cat rescues from trees our in-house joke was, "Have you ever seen a cat skeleton in a tree?" On our crew we always called upon Grant for this task. He had two cats as pets making him best suited for this. He would don his turnout coat and gloves; some cats can be rather feisty when encountered by Grant standing on a ladder or in the bucket of the tower ladder. I understand now that in his long career, he rescued sixteen cats and one Sandhill Crane. Grant was not only a talented cat rescuer; he had many skills. He was very mechanically inclined and very reliable. If a commander or lieutenant had a specific or involved task, Grant was the firefighter they could count on to get the job done.

Another talented crew member was Joe Samillano. Before becoming Lieutenant Samillano, he was at the rank of firefighter. We once responded to a call to assist a tree trimmer who was dangling from a large tree behind a home on Noble Place. It appeared he was working alone and might have tried tackling more than he could handle by himself.

Equipment dispatched to respond was Engine 5, Rescue 1, Tower Ladder 1, and a command chief. Noble place was in a quaint older section of downtown Orlando. The streets were quite narrow and at that time were paved with bricks. Engine 5 was the first to arrive and reported a man was hanging upside down about 30 feet off the ground. As we turned left off of Mills Avenue onto Noble Place, we could see to our right the tree trimmer behind the first corner house that faced Mills Avenue. He was dangling from the north side of the tree; this would be to our advantage.

A large water oak tree branch was hanging perpendicular across his lower abdomen and upper legs, pinning him against the tree. His pain was intense and losing awareness from dangling upside down. A voice was heard saying that we needed a 35-foot extension ladder. A 35-foot ladder would reach him, but it would be unstable to work from, plus only one firefighter, maybe two, would be able to work from below the tree trimmer. We needed to support his upper body, getting him somewhat upright. The limb would also have to be moved upward and outward to rescue him.

Hearing this Joe said, "Let's use the bucket." The lieutenant agreed, and we went to work. Our assigned lieutenant that day was off, so a lieutenant off an engine company was sent to ride in charge. He was a respected and competent company officer, but since this rescue would evolve the use of the tower ladder, he felt comfortable having Joe take the lead.

The distance from the street to the large water oak tree was just out of the booms reach, so Joe suggested we back it in. To work directly off the back of the truck was one of the most stable for an aerial operation, especially when off road.

We had a few obstacles to contend with when turning and backing in the 45-foot fire truck, but we felt certain we had enough room. With Joe at the rear of the apparatus, I had complete confidence he would guide the truck with exact precision. I backed up a few feet to make a hard left into the driveway across the street. I had to drive up and into the yard to swing the truck ninety degrees or perpendicular to the street. In doing so the weight of the truck left deep ruts from the front tires. But we weren't concerned, as the yard could be repaired. I Immediately went to my left mirror and saw Joe. All I had to do is keep the side of the truck centered on Joe and whatever way he moved I adjusted the truck accordingly. We had been in similar situations that required such backing, and Joe was not only conscious of the situation at hand but also what was going on around him. The truck climbed the low curb with no problem and back we went, making small adjustments. When Joe's hands made a fist, I stopped the truck, and he gave me a thumbs up. I set the emergency air brake.

After switching the PTO (power take-off) lever to the on position, I quickly climbed down from the cab. My first action would be to move around to the front of the truck and look for any obstructions on the right side that might hinder the outrigger stabilization jack from fully extending. This was my first real look at how well Joe did. It was a tight fit, but, like always, he did an excellent job. I noticed a mound of dirt next to the right outrigger jack and was fairly certain this jack would not be able to be fully extend. Moving back to the left side, I opened the compartment door that housed the controls to operate each of the four stabilization jacks. If there were no obstructions, both front outrigger jacks could be extended at the same time, but since the right outrigger had an obstruction it would have to be supervised. The responsibility of the firefighter riding behind me was to set the flat aluminum stabilization pads on the right side of the truck. He would communicate to me how far the jack could be extended and still place the ground pad beneath it. If an outrigger jack cannot be fully extended outwards, the tower boom is restricted on how far it can work from that side of the truck. The bucket could not extend farther than the jack extends outward, greatly limiting the reach of the bucket. Joe knew the limitations of our apparatus, and because we were working off road on possible unstable ground, he positioned the truck in a straight line with the victim. In this way, we were hopeful not to have to move the bucket to the left. The area on my side of the truck was unobstructed. I only had to place the pads under each stabilization jack and raise the truck, transferring the weight from the truck's tires to its four jacks.

I next turned on electrical power to the bucket and moved the hydraulic lever that had previously operated the jacks so it would operate the boom. The lieutenant and Joe were in the bucket and started up. Joe, at the controls, made quick work getting to the conscious victim. He carefully guided the bucket up and underneath the hanging upside-down man allowing the lieutenant to wrap his arms underneath the victim's arms and around his chest, securing him. Joe then slowly raised the bucket, raising the man upward, still cradled in the lieutenant's arms. The victim was far from comfortable, but he was supported by the lieutenant, which clearly relieved some of his pain. This was also uncomfortable for the lieutenant, but he had the bucket railing to assist him.

Because the lieutenant was involved with patient care, Joe had to take over rescue operations. He immediately turned off the electrical power that operated the bucket controls. If accidentally activated, these bucket controls could cause further injury to the victim or potential injury to the rescuers. Joe made a quick evaluation of the situation and correctly determined the heavy limb would have to be raised up and out to free him.

I quickly climbed the ladder attached to the top of the boom and stood on the back railing of the bucket. From my vantage point, I could see the rope was attached to the limb, which he would use to lower it after it was cut. But then something went wrong. The rope had somehow wrapped itself around the large limb that was pinning the tree trimmer.

Using a clove hitch, Joe tied a rope around the cut end of this limb. He told me to set up a pulley system using a large limb above their heads as an anchor. I doubled a section of ½-inch nylon utility rope that was kept in the bucket. Looping it around the overhead limb, I secured both ends using a square knot tied as close to the limb as possible. I then hooked a steel carabiner to it. Taking Joe's rope, I clipped it through the carabiner and hoped I could pull down with enough force to raise the limb. Unfortunately, I was unsuccessful, and we had no pulleys or mechanical advantages at that time. Joe, thankfully, was able to help so we could finally lift the limb successfully. As the limb moved upward it also moved outward, releasing its hold on the tree trimmer.

Joe would now need to help the lieutenant with the victim. He asked if I could hold the load as he slowly released his grip. It turned out I could, which gave Joe and the lieutenant time to upright the victim and reposition him in a girl carry in the lieutenant's arms. Joe quickly took the end of the rope I was holding and secured it around the end of the branch so it didn't fall. I moved back to the back railing of the bucket, and Joe lowered everyone to the ground.

The paramedics on both Rescue 1 and the ambulance quickly installed a traction splint to each of the man's legs to relieve pain. He had broken both femur bones but had no other injuries. He would go through numerous operations involving rods and screws, but eventually he would fully recover.

Overall, the entire operation went well, and all involved were highly commended, especially Joe Samillano for his quick thinking. He would later become a lieutenant and be assigned to Tower Ladder 1. Anyone who had the opportunity to work with Joe was fortunate to have him as their company officer.

• • •

Not long after this rescue, the Orlando Fire Department hired two excellent firefighters, who had numerous years with the Altamonte Springs Fire Department north of Orlando. They both were intelligent, fit, and strong. Larry Arthur brought his knowledge and expertise in rope rescue. He believed passionately that all firefighters should have a personal rescue rope bag attached to their breathing apparatus. A rescue rope could be easily deployed should a firefighter be trapped and needed to exit a window or balcony. Larry was also instrumental in establishing the Orlando Fire Department High Angle Rescue Team. Once again, the department was moving forward with increasing professionalism, in the spirit of the safety of their firefighters and the citizens of Orlando.

Larry had relatives on the FDNY and considered a job with them. He took the test and scored number one, which was quite a feat seeing that over ten thousand candidates took the test. Just like with Joe, the city of Orlando was fortunate to have Larry as a member of its fire department. I had the opportunity to work with some outstanding firefighters in my career, and Larry was certainly one of them.

Another great talent was Mike Aiken from Altamonte Springs Fire Department. He worked with Larry to get the rope program up and running, and he, like Larry, was an excellent instructor. I always wished I'd had their verbal communication skills.

One clear sunny morning Larry and Mike were training our newly formed high angle team at the Altamonte Springs water tower. The team would practice their repelling skills from the top of the 145-foot tower. Inside the base of the tower was a steel ladder that extended straight up and through the center of the water tank, exiting on top of the dome-shaped lid. To gain access to its top, each trainee would have to climb the 145-foot ladder. For safety, a third solid rail was secured at the center point between the two ladder rails. This rail had a steel ascender permanently attached to it. Each climber attached their repelling harness to the ascender with a carabiner; if they slipped or became tired, the harness would automatically catch them or support them so they could rest.

As each climber ascended, the steel ascender produced a clacking noise as it ran along its sprocket edge. The sound was amplified by the enclosed steel cylindrical structure that supported the water tank. The speed of the firefighter's ascent would determine the tempo of the clacking. Most climbers' tempos greatly slow as they got higher on the ladder and often stop when the climber was in need of rest. To climb 145 feet straight up with 14 inches between each step is a great climb. But not for Mike. When he started at floor level, he produced a tempo that mimicked a machine gun, and it didn't stop until he reached the top. There was no one in our group who could come close to duplicating this feat. Mike, like Larry, was a sound competent firefighter and would advance through the ranks, retiring as a district chief.

. . .

The fire department also saw the need to implement a hazardous material response team. Hazardous materials were getting a lot of attention, and many larger departments were putting together a response team. I knew this would be expensive as it required in-depth training for those on the team. Station 1 would be the home for this team. The personnel of Engine 101 (formally known as Engine 51), along with the Rescue 1 and Tower Ladder 1 teams, would be trained in this highly technical endeavor. I found some of this technical training to be quite difficult to grasp, but we had firefighters who were very intelligent in this area, and I was comforted knowing we had such outstanding folks on the team.

A truck was purchased to house the vast equipment needed for hazardous material calls. It would be parked behind Engine 101 and when a hazardous material call was received it would also respond. Hazardous material calls could be quite involved and take many hours, sometimes days, to mitigate and, hopefully, resolve.

My first major hazardous material call involved an overturned gasoline tanker truck. The 8,000-gallon tractor trailer was heading east on Interstate 4 just north of Church Street when it swerved to avoid hitting an aluminum ladder that had fallen off a truck. This poorly secured 12-foot light duty ladder would cause major problems for the fire department and commuters. The tanker truck driver, desperately wanting to avoid hitting the ladder flying toward his truck, swerved and, as a result, the weight of the trailer caused the truck to turn over. It came to rest on its left side on the inside lane of this four-lane east bound highway.

This accident happened on C shift on a weekday evening. They responded quickly and, under the command of Lieutenant David Barker, went right to work. Since fire was a concern, foam hose lines were stretched. One of the full compartments of gasoline was ripped open, causing the entire amount to spill onto the interstate. The team worked quickly to contain the escaping fuel by using booms. They also requested a load of sand be brought to the scene and applied dome clamps to the tanker fill lids that were on their sides and leaking gasoline. Some of the fuel had made its way to storm drains that led to Lake Lucerne. Firefighters responded to the west side of Lake Lucerne and set up a floating boom to try to contain the gasoline.

The next morning when I arrived at work, we relieved the previous shift on the scene. With the C shift having the scene secure, we began the process of off-loading the fuel to another tanker truck so the truck could be righted.

We would be attempting a fairly new innovation at that time. Since the tanker was on its side, the petroleum exit valves were inaccessible and damaged. We would drill a 3¾-inch-diameter hole through the aluminum skin on the tank. A hose would be inserted, and the remaining gasoline would be pumped to the recovery truck. Since this technique was new at the time, there was an air of tension. Lieutenant David Barker and Lieutenant Tom Kelly, the two shift hazardous material commanders, would perform this dangerous task.

These two lieutenants sat on top of the tanker and, using an air operated hole saw, drilled through the $\frac{3}{16}$-inch-thick aluminum. A foam hose line flowed foam over the area being drilled, plus a foam monitor nozzle rained foam down on top of them. Red Huber would take a spectacular photograph of this operation. Everything went well and was safely completed. Two large Class C wreckers would use heavy nylon straps to right the truck.

All told, Interstate 4 had been closed down for almost twenty-four hours, but if the tanker truck had caught fire, it may have been closed for months. All agencies did a superb job, and I was quite proud of our department.

. . .

One service we provided the citizens of Orlando was to control water leaks inside of structures. This service was performed by the ladder companies that would respond nonemergency and, if possible, shut off the flow of water. Depending on the situation, we would also help remove collected water from the structure.

One early Saturday morning around 1:30 a.m., we responded to a water salvage at a two-story apartment complex on East Michigan Street. The caller, a woman in her thirties, who occupied an apartment on the ground floor, met us at her front door. She politely asked us if we could possibly be quiet because her two young daughters were sleeping on two sofas in the small living room, and her husband, who was sick, was sleeping in the only bedroom.

She had turned on a small lamp on the kitchen counter to illuminate the area of the living room—too dim to wake the children. We were fine with that, as we always come equipped with our personal flashlights. She then advised us that water was dripping from the ceiling in the living room. We noticed two places where water was coming through the drywall but luckily not at an alarming rate. The children weren't getting wet, but one arm of one sofa was, so we simply picked up the small sofa as the child slept and moved it to a dry location.

The lieutenant sent me to the apartment directly above to evaluate where the water was coming from. No one was home but, thankfully, the door was unlocked. It turned out the occupant had not completely turned off the cold water in the bathroom sink in which a shirt had blocked the overflow drain causing the sink to overflow and make its way to the apartment below. I turned the water completely off, removed the shirt, and placed it in the bathtub. Luckily there was only a small amount of damage to both apartments.

When I returned to the first-floor apartment, I noticed numerous prescription medicine bottles on the kitchen counter and empty oxygen bottles next to the front door. I also noticed when we'd moved the sofa that the entire room was filled with furniture, making it almost impossible to move around. It looked to me like they had way too much furniture for such a small apartment. Something just didn't seem right.

By this time, we had everything in order and the lieutenant returned to the truck to start writing his report. The other two crew members were conversing with four young ladies who had just returned from a party. I climbed up into the driver's seat, but something stirred inside of me. I said to the lieutenant, "I'll be right back." He gave me no mind, nor did other crew members, as I made my way back to the apartment. I lightly knocked on the front door and the woman let me back in. I told her I didn't want to pry, but I told her what I had noticed and felt moved to ask. She explained her husband had cancer and, due to medical bills, they'd had to sell their home and move into the apartment. As we talked in the dimly lit kitchen I felt such compassion for this family. To see her daughters peacefully sleeping in the dark cluttered living room and know her husband was dying in the bedroom was heartbreaking. I told her how sad and sorry I was for their situation. I reached into my front pocket and handed her my neatly folded cash and said I hope this would help in some way. From her tired worn-out self, she thanked me, and I walked back to the truck.

Incidents like this one have stayed with me all these years. I've been involved in some interesting and dangerous scenes, but I seem to be moved more by these unglamorous, but memorable, incidents.

I remember the rescue of Jim in the late winter and receiving quite a bit of attention for a few months. Yet that very same year we responded to a house fire on the evening of Christmas. The fire came in around 8:00 p.m., on East Esther Street. On arrival, moderate smoke was blanketing the dark residential street. Engine Company 5, had pulled one 1¾-inch hose line through the front door. The smoke wasn't too heavy, but a mask was required. The fire was the result of a bunched up electrical blanket on a bed that was left on. The occupants had left the house to visit neighbors and when they returned their home was filled with smoke. Engine 5 quickly made their way to the seat of the fire and extinguished the smoldering blanket.

Searching the house for occupants, I found a lethargic puppy under a bed and took him outside. The puppy was starting to come around, but I took him to Rescue 1 where Paul Nutting, a paramedic, administered oxygen to its small snoot. He was about the same size as Toby, the dog I'd resuscitated at the Beggs Avenue fire. I notice a small boy looking on, and I signaled to him, pointing to the small dog, wondering if it was his puppy. It turned out it was. The puppy had been given to him as a Christmas present earlier that day. By then the dog seemed fine so I handed it back to the child who immediately snuggled the puppy to his face, holding him tightly.

So, in the same year, I had rescued both a human being (Jim) and a small puppy. Not that the rescue of Jim wasn't important, but I will admit the rescue of this small dog and being able to hand it back to its young owner had a great impact on me. I can still see the face of the boy, maybe 20 feet away, looking around with sorrow and concern for his puppy. Yet I have trouble remembering Jim's face. The smoke was heavy, and I was working frantically. An interesting side note: Jim's rescue was on a weekday afternoon with media on the scene, so pictures of the incident and the rescue were in the newspaper the next day. With the puppy rescue on Christmas night, most photographers and media weren't working, but were home with their loved ones. Though the puppy rescue would have made for good news, it went unnoticed, but certainly not by me nor the little boy. Once again, those small insignificant events have shaped the person I am today, and I'm extremely thankful.

. . .

The morning of January 28, 1986, was quite cold for Orlando. I had just backed the tower ladder into its bay and pushed the engine stop. I started walking to the back door of the firehouse to watch the launch of the space shuttle Challenger. As I neared the back of the apparatus floor the bell rang. Stopping to listen to what units were being dispatched, Engineer-Paramedic Dewey Speegle came up to me. He'd been outside watching the launch and had seen the space shuttle explode! At that very moment we were dispatched to a house fire on East Winter Park Street next to Interstate 4. We turned right out of the firehouse, left onto South Street, and then onto the ramp to Interstate 4 heading north. Around Lake Concord I could see directly in front of us a fairly dense column of black smoke making its way skyward. Looking to my right and leaning forward to see out the lieutenant's window, I saw the twisted vapor trails of the Challenger.

We exited off the interstate at the Princeton Street exit, went left under the interstate, first right on Formosa Avenue, up four streets, and then a right onto East Winter Park Street. The small wood-framed house was on the north side of the street.

As I set the air brake, I saw from my driver's side window, fire pushing out of the top of a large bedroom window on the east side of the house. Grant Aiello was our "outside ventilation" man, so he took this window first. As I trailed behind Grant, I saw Lieutenant Bob Pearce from Engine 3 and his nozzle man bleed the air from the hose, donning masks to prepare for entrance. Lieutenant Joe Samillano and his forcible entry man were forcing the front door with the Halligan and axe.

When Grant thrust his Halligan hook through the eastward facing window he caught the top of the inside portion of the window, and with one pull the entire window and its frame came out, crashing to the ground. This now large ventilation opening would relieve heat and smoke buildup from the bedroom. As I walked around to the back door, I overheard Chief Alan MacAllaster say to Grant, "Nice vent."

I entered through the back door with Grant behind me. We searched the back of this small structure while Lieutenant Joe and the forcible entry man made quick work of the front half. An all clear was reported, and I went to the fire bedroom to assist with overhaul. There I met up with Lieutenant Bob and his nozzle man squatting on their knees, taking a short break. I asked Lieutenant Bob if he'd heard about the space shuttle explosion. He said he hadn't, and I could see in his eyes, through his mask, that he wasn't sure if I was making it up or not. I only had to point out the large opening Grant produced. With the fire's smoke rapidly clearing, we could see out into the dark blue sky the whitish brown vapor trails from the explosion still visible. His eyes went from wonder to sadness, and what a truly sad day it was.

. . .

We had just finished the evening meal when the communications sections said over the PA system, "Everyone goes." The alarm was transmitted for a fire at the Broadway United Methodist Church. Units responding from our firehouse were both engine companies, the tower ladder, Rescue Company 1, and two command chiefs. Being a weekday evening, our response was quite rapid. Upon arrival we saw no indication of fire and were met by the chief of the department, Gene Reynolds, who was attending a meeting at the church. He met with Engine 1's officer and advised there was a fire in the basement, pointing to the open basement door. Engine 1's driver Tim Sachse, mindful, pulled up far enough to allow the tower ladder to position itself in the most advantageous place for aerial operations. We now had "good scrub area," meaning the bucket would be able to freely move without being obstructed by other apparatuses, power poles, etc. This was most important if the bucket was needed to reach windows for rescue. Engine 1's crew pulled a hose line from their truck and advanced it toward the open door that was now emitting smoke. Engine 101 brought in a large diameter water supply hose line and hooked it into Engine 1. Engine 101 would then return to the hydrant, hook up to the hydrant, and increase volume and pressure to Engine 1 by pumping the water through its pump. That way, numerous hand lines could be pulled off of Engine 1 without decreasing the pressure of the other hose lines. Tower Ladder 1's crew entered the building along with the advancing hose line, and it was quickly determined that we had a serious fire and it had extended inside the back wall, opposite the sanctuary wall, and to the upper floors. The ladder company officer reported this information to the chief in command, who quickly transmitted a second alarm. Engine 101's crew pulled another attack hose line from Engine 1 and advanced it to the first floor, just over the basement. We now had a good volume of smoke coming from the windows over the basement area so the outside ventilation man, along with the crew of Rescue 1, ventilated only those windows. We knew heat was building in the sanctuary because the stained glass windows were making a crackling noise, but, so far, the fire hadn't got into the sanctuary. If we could keep the fire out of the sanctuary, we would save the church and its large, beautiful stain glass windows.

I was taught large church or cathedral fires were challenging because of the large open sanctuary, heavy timber construction, and wood pews and trim, along with heavy coats of combustible finishes. Plus because of the height, steepness, and heavy construction of the roof system, roof ventilation was virtually impossible. But it appeared the fire was staying in the three-story building attached to the front of the sanctuary. It hadn't extended into the sanctuary, though it was moving upward rapidly.

If we could get to the roof and make an opening over the main body of fire, we had a chance of channeling the fire upward and out of the building, possibly keeping it from moving horizontally. It should also relieve the heat buildup allowing the engine companies to advance their hose lines to the seat of the fire for extinguishment. With more companies making their way to the scene and hand lines being stretched, Tower Ladder 1 was making their way to the roof. One obstacle they encountered was a steel cable stretching from one telephone pole to another directly above the apparatus. Luckily Jerry Troutman, a lineman with the Orlando Utility Commission was on the scene. He quickly removed the cable, letting the tower ladder's boom raise high enough to reach the roof of the three-story building.

With Tower Ladder 1 on the roof, they used their K1200 power saw to cut a 4 x 4-foot opening in the roof. As the saw easily cut through the rolled roofing, the firefighter used a Halligan hook to remove the wood sheeting. Black dense smoke, under pressure, rapidly escaped. Seconds later this smoke turned to a square block of fire extending 6 to 8 feet into the air. This block of fire produced a tremendous amount of light that lit up the roof and branches of the live oak trees that canopied the church. The roof team knew they had produced a good ventilation opening and hoped it would help keep the fire from extending horizontally and, more importantly, relieve the intense beating the engine and ladder companies were taking on the fire floors.

With the fire exiting the building, somewhat like a massive chimney, it allowed cooler outside air to be drawn through the ventilated windows, lowering the intense heat, allowing the firefighters to advance to the seat of the fire. With numerous hose lines advanced to all floors and the ladder companies opening up the walls and ceilings, the destructive dangerous fire was brought under control.

We encountered some problems at this fire that we had to overcome, but if it wasn't for the aggressiveness of the firefighters and the knowledge of the incident commander, we may have lost Broadway Methodist Church and its beautiful stained-glass windows.

Once again, I was proud of our department, we were a large team, working together for a common goal. Assistant Chief Mike Kelly was in command of the fire; his sector command chiefs worked well together to deploy these units safely and efficiently.

With numerous companies at the fire the communications section was also extremely busy. Their efforts were rarely acknowledged, but they had the very important job of monitoring the fire, and they quickly responded to any request a commander might need. They had to relocate apparatus to stations that needed coverage, and, on top of everything, they were often required to handle a heavy emergency call load from every

corner of the city. I certainly considered them unsung heroes, and still do
to this day.

.   .   .

In the early 1980s, the Orlando Fire Department hired two female firefighters, along with others hired soon after. They were pioneers, so to
speak. There were male firefighters who were quite upset. Some would
not acknowledge them, even to the point of not speaking to them. I don't
know to what extent, but they took verbal and sexual abuse. There would
be some changes around the firehouse. One was that all firefighters were
issued blue shorts with the fire department emblem screenprinted on the
right pant leg. There would be no more sleeping naked or in underwear.
In some firehouses, a sign was affixed to the bathroom door to indicate
if a female was inside. Firefighting gear, such as turnout coats, pants, and
boots were all made for men. These first female firefighters had to put
up with turnout gear that didn't fit well, but in time firefighting turnout
gear and dress uniforms were made to fit females as well. Until that time,
they had to put up with the inconvenience and the dangers of ill-fitting
protective gear. I admired their fortitude and grit.

.   .   .

At this point, I had been in the department for a while, experiencing different emergencies and gaining experience. I didn't know it at the time,
but I was becoming proud, and a little too sure of myself. I hope I didn't
project an arrogance—sometimes just the way we carry ourselves, without saying a word, can radiate an arrogance.

One morning around 9:30 we responded with Engine Company 5,
Rescue 2, and a command chief. A construction worker had fallen into an
open excavation pit and broken his leg. When we arrived on the scene engineer-paramedic Paul Nutting and Firefighter-Paramedic Jeanne Potter
from Rescue 2, as well as firefighters off of Engine Company 5 had the
victim's leg in a splint and were securing him in a stokes basket. Our assignment was to use the tower ladder's aerial boom to lift the patient from
the bottom of the pit. The basket would have to be secured to the underside of the boom using a harness and then lifted to ground level where

an ambulance was waiting. The problem we encountered was the nylon harness straps weren't to be found; they weren't in their assigned location. The victim wasn't in any distress and didn't need to be expedited to the hospital. In fact, we had enough firefighters and construction workers to form a human chain in order to pass the patient up the steep bank. But the safest and smoothest way was to use the aerial boom.

I thought I would remember how to tie a Spanish bowline that I'd been taught many years before in a rope class. It was used for just such a purpose. I remember the instructor giving us this very same scenario, one in which we misplaced the harness straps. With the command chief giving me the go-ahead, I secured a rope, and down into the pit I went. I started strong, weaving the rope correctly through each side of the basket and now had the lifting harness, or sling, portion finished. But that's when I found myself at a loss. With this one rope making the four lifting points on the basket, I now had a total of three ⅝-inch ropes lying across my open left hand. I tried numerous times to manipulate these ropes to form the correct knot but was unsuccessful each time. This was extremely embarrassing for myself, the firefighters, the chief, and the department I so dearly loved. My actions were making all look unprofessional and that alone bothered me the most. On top of everything, the construction workers were getting vocal with my folly, and I could understand why. They were concerned for their brother just as we would be for our brothers and sisters in a similar situation.

I knew I had failed, and directed the crew to pass the injured man up the incline. I assisted with passing the patient and all went well. We loaded him into the waiting ambulance and off they went to the hospital just down the street. We then started searching for the missing harness. We eventually found them haphazardly thrown in the back of the wrong compartment. Though I was the engineer of the truck, this was my responsibility that all equipment was accounted for and in its correct location.

So, needless to say, I was very disappointed in myself that morning. I felt terrible the entire shift, and thought about this incident for months, reliving my poor performance and my responsibilities as an engineer. But over this lengthy soul-searching evaluation, I finely came to the realization that I had been prideful. Prideful by definition means to have an excessively high opinion of oneself. I didn't feel I had an excessively high opinion, but I knew I had some measure. I also knew God dislikes even a small amount of pride in a person, so maybe this was my wake-up call. It was a humbling incident; it cut into my importance. It took me almost a year to share how I felt about this with others, but now I'm freely able to do so, as I understand the danger of even a little pride.

• • •

When it came to first aid calls, we on the tower ladder at Station 1 felt somewhat weak. For us to be dispatched to a first-aid call, both engine companies and the rescue company would have to be tied up on a call. This rarely happened, so we rarely responded to a first aid call. The problem with not responding to at least a few first aid calls is you become rusty and unsure of yourself. You just don't feel comfortable with the task at hand, and that's obviously not a good situation. We knew our shortcomings and, usually, we had at least one firefighter who was fairly proficient on first aid scenes. We could bandage and splint, take blood pressures, pulse, etc, but setting up different IVs, helping the paramedics with administering drugs, or dealing with a combative or unconscious person were not our strong suits.

Though confessing this now, I'm happy to share that we had one afternoon call that proved we could still do our jobs well. We were returning to quarters at noon time and were at the intersection of Orange Avenue and Central Boulevard.

A woman flagged us down to a person unconscious at a restaurant on the corner. I pulled the truck in front of the restaurant, turned on the emergency lights and rushed inside with my team. The crowd told us that a man was having a heart attack and pointed to a Federal Express delivery man lying on his back. We quickly determined he wasn't breathing and didn't have a pulse. Roger Herota checked for an obstruction but found none, then repositioned his head and was handed a bag mask. I started chest compressions while Lieutenant Samillano notified our communications section. They immediately sent Rescue 1 to our location.

Luckily Rescue 1 was coming from quarters and would arrive quickly. We continued to do CPR and felt we were doing a good job. Rescue 1 arrived along with the ambulance company. Engineer-paramedic Dewey Speegle and Firefighter-Paramedic John Williams from Rescue 1 started their standard protocol. Rescue 1 and the paramedics off the ambulance took over. We helped them load the victim into the ambulance and off they went to the hospital.

When Rescue 1 returned to quarters, they were pleased to report the FedEx driver was doing well. In fact, he returned to work, and we would often see him around town; he'd always greet us with a smile and say thanks. The reason he survived, we were told, was because we initiated CPR so quickly, but I'm sure Dewey, John, the ambulance paramedics, and emergency room workers had a lot to do with it.

I personally felt bad not helping with the late-night barrage of medical calls. On a Friday or Saturday night, usually after 12:00 a.m. the city could get quite busy, especially in the downtown area. The engine companies along with the rescues would be running from one call to another while we were tucked in our beds. Though, on those busy nights, I usually woke when the tower ladder was the remaining apparatus to respond to a medical call. One such Saturday night, around 1:30 a.m., the communications section announced Tower 1." We rolled out of bed as the alarm was sounding. We were dispatched with Rescue 2 for an "Obstetrics in progress," at the east side of Lake Eola Park. An OB in progress was the type of medical emergency we were least comfortable dealing with. As we turned right onto East Central Boulevard, Lieutenant Joe asked what rescue company was responding. I told him Rescue 2, and he said, "Thank goodness." We were fortunate to have the busiest rescue company responding with us. Engineer-paramedic Paul Nutting had delivered numerous babies; in fact, by the time he retired, he had assisted with twenty-six live births. His partner was Firefighter-Paramedic Jeanne Potter, and she also had numerous deliveries to her credit, which, on that night, was comforting to know. We just hoped they arrived soon. We arrived at the park and saw no indication of a woman in distress. Lieutenant Joe contacted communications and relayed our situation. They informed us they had no further information. In the end, it turned out to be a false alarm, and we were much relieved. I'm also sure Rescue 2 had a good laugh at us sweating bullets over the call.

Speaking about medical calls and responding to first aids . . . When I came on the department, we were taught the American Red Cross first-aid course. It wasn't very in-depth, but this was 1971. The EMT as a professional role was fairly new, and only a few firefighters were certified. When I rode with engineer Bob Shawen, an EMT, I considered taking the course but felt it may be too in-depth and with my poor reading and comprehension skills I wasn't sure I would do well. But when I found a home on the ladder truck and was getting more and more fascinated with the techniques of firefighting, the medical side of the department didn't hold the same fascination. In the early 1970s the city went with the 911 emergency call system. Even back when I came on, a lot of our emergencies were medical in nature and advanced first aid training was needed. When paramedics came on the scene in the mid 1970s, Paul Nutting and Dewey Speegle were in the first classes. I mention these two because other firefighters in our department were also in these first classes, but I worked with Paul and Dewey most of my career. Some members may have felt I didn't support the paramedic program, but I felt the fire department was best suited to provide this service. It was a win-win for the residents of Orlando and the department.

Throughout my career I had been on the scene with paramedics many times, but because I was always assigned to Tower Ladder 1, I rarely had an opportunity to see them performing their life-saving expertise at medical calls.

One weekday I was assigned to ride in the officer's position of the tower ladder. We were returning to quarters from a call, in Station 5's response area when our communications section asked our location. They dispatched us along with Rescue 1 to a cardiac call. We all arrived at the single-family dwelling at the same time. We would assist engineer-paramedic Ray Taylor and Firefighter-Paramedic Ray Alonge with their vast medical equipment. An elderly lady met us at the front door and quickly took us to her husband who was lying on the den floor. My job would be to write down the drugs used and the times they were administered.

The two Rays immediately went to work, with professionalism and unassuming confidence. CPR was started, EKG leads were applied, the endotracheal tube was precisely guided down the trachea, IV lines were setup and started, and the defibrillator was powered up and at the ready. The mans' wife stood close to me in the doorway while I held the clipboard in my flexed arm making notes. She had wrapped her right hand under my left arm for support and, I think, comfort. I leaned my head down to the elderly wife, who was wrapped in a long light-pink robe, and quietly told her that the paramedics were doing everything possible for her husband. She whispered, "I know," in a sorrowful tone. That cold morning, I witnessed two highly trained and skilled paramedics, along with other dedicated firefighters, diligently working to save a life. Once again, I was extremely proud of our department and the services we provided for the citizens of Orlando.

I now wonder all of these years later, if the wife, standing so close to me, was recalling not that scary night, but instead beautiful memories of her and her husband together. Maybe an intimate time together, or uncontrollable laughter over a funny experience, or maybe their smiling love for the birth of a child. I hoped it all boiled down to a deep love and respect for one another.

I'm pleased to add that after their retirement from the department, the two Rays went on to continue helping humanity. Ray Taylor continued facilitating and teaching paramedic courses at the same college he'd helped years prior to get a paramedic program established. What better person to teach paramedic classes than Ray having over twenty-five years at a busy company? He's very smart in the field of emergency medicine and an excellent instructor.

Ray Alonge went back to school; his next career was as a nurse anesthetist. I'm proud of them both. It was an honor to have worked with them.

. . .

The ladder companies were responsible for handling elevator emergencies. With no actual training in the operation of elevators, we would have to learn this on our own. There were some publications on operation and safety procedures for this, but we wanted and needed more information on these lifting and lowering devices. When out on company inspection—I personally didn't care for the term "company inspection." I felt "company survey," or "building familiarity," were better terms to use when meeting a business owner or manager. The fire department and the owner were to work together to make their building as safe as possible. The word "inspection" already feels slightly threatening and to get on the wrong side of a business owner can cause animosity—so, when out on *building familiarity*, and we happened to encounter an elevator repair person, we would pick their brains to learn more about elevators. These experts were usually very helpful and willing to share their information. After learning more, we encountered two somewhat different problems that we would have to deal with. Elevator rescue, or occupant removal, was one thing, but gaining control of an elevator at a fire was another.

We became quite proficient at occupant rescue. We wrote SOPs, so each crew member knew their assignment, tools to carry, and location to report to. Each morning at the start of our twenty-four-hour shift, the company officer would assign the different duties to each of our four crew members. This information was now added to the duty roster along with the duties for the water rescue team, hazardous material team, and high angle team.

At Firehouse 1, we often responded to elevator emergencies because our house was centrally located downtown where more multistory buildings were located. We alone responded to these calls, but if an occupant was having any medical problems a rescue company would accompany us.

One weekday morning we responded to an obstetrics in progress at the Orlando Public Library. It was before opening, and eight or so librarians were inside the elevator. The elevator car was stuck between the basement and the first floor. The quickest access into the elevator car was through the top, or roof, hatch. We quickly opened the first-floor elevator hoist-way doors and secured the electrical power. The top of the car was level with the first floor, so we simply walked onto the top of the car and opened the hatch. We then lowered an attic ladder down through the opening, and one member of Rescue 1's crew entered the car. It was quickly evaluated that the young pregnant woman wasn't in any distress, and all were relieved. We advised the occupants they had two choices to exit the car. One was to climb the ladder and exit through the top and out onto the first floor. The other was to wait while we lowered the car to the basement. Being a hydraulic operated elevator, we could lower the car by rerouting the hydraulic fluid, to help the car move slowly downward.

By now there was some bantering between the firefighters and librarians. I know from experience that most librarians are extremely intelligent, quick witted, and just plain cool. I overheard one say, "You know how those firefighters are. They want us to use the ladder so they can look at our butts." I couldn't stop laughing.

One other memorable elevator call was at the Raddison Hotel. If I recall correctly, they had four banks of elevators, but one elevator, second from the right, would malfunction due to being overloaded with too many occupants. If we received an alarm on a Friday or Saturday night, late in the evening, we were quite certain we knew which elevator bank was involved. And this Saturday night's alarm was no exception.

Upon arrival, management met us and confirmed it was the second from the right elevator, and it was probably overloaded due to a gathering for a ten-year high school reunion. The elevator was packed with young women who had been drinking, and definitely having a good time.

That day's shift, Firefighter Larry Arthur was assigned to the rescue position. He would be the person, if needed, to repel down the elevator shaft to reach the elevator's top hatch. We were able to gain access from the floor above as I secured the electrical power to this cable-drawn elevator. Once the power was turned off, Larry climbed on top of the car and opened the hatch cover. Larry introduced himself and advised the ladies to be aware he was about to lower a folding attic ladder down into the car. Larry, who just happened to be quite handsome, descended the ladder. Once inside the car, numerous young ladies started vying to be rescued by Larry. I could hear the conversation between these lively ladies and Larry. Larry was not only handsome but funny with quick comebacks. The ladies and Larry were enjoying the situation, and I began to wonder if they actually wanted to be rescued. Slowly the first young lady emerged from the opening.

This cable-drawn elevator had a steel I-beam running the width of the car about 16 inches above the car. The occupants would have to navigate over this beam to exit the top of the car, an area that could be quite dark, dirty, and greasy. Since the ladies were finely dressed, Lieutenant Samillano was not only concerned for their footing, since some were wearing high heels, but also their nice clothing. He felt it would be best to pick up each lady in a girl carry and pass her over the beam into the arms of Firefighter Gerry Kasper, who was quite willing to help in any way he could. Securely holding each young lady, Gerry slowly lowered them to the floor lobby. One after the other congregated in the lobby area outside the elevator talking and laughing. One had her red plastic drink cup secured in her teeth while her arms were wrapped securely around the firefighter's. There were about fifteen ladies total that we rescued from the elevator. When they got to me, in the lobby, one lady said, "I got to pee, thank you." The perks of being a firefighter.

We encountered one other problem when it came to our procedures around elevators. We'd get a fire alarm transmitted from a high-rise building or even a low-rise multistory building. The elevators in those buildings were vital to transport us and our equipment to the fire. If the fire was reported below the tenth floor, we would take the interior stairwell; if it was happening above the tenth floor, we used the elevator, but we could only use it if it was equipped with a fire service feature, so we could manually operate it. To do that, we needed a special key. And if there were multiple elevator banks, that meant we needed a unique key for each. Each elevator company also had unique keys for their particular brand and style of elevator

What we did was ask an elevator repairman from the company if he would give us a key. We would then, if possible, have it duplicated for each crew member on our truck. Some keys were stamped with the words do not duplicate; if so, some key-makers were hesitant to duplicate it and may not have the blank needed with which to duplicate it. At that time in my career, this became quite frustrating when we needed an elevator for an emergency. I personally set out to acquire as many different keys as I could and, when I retired, I had eighteen keys for all the different manufacturers of elevators. Even with this well-labeled set of keys, I still had trouble accessing some elevators, because an elevator may say it's a Dover or Westinghouse, but Otis elevator had taken over the maintenance and service of the elevator and changed the fire service keyway to accept their Otis key. So sometimes I had to try different keys hoping one would work.

One universal key would solve this problem and we lobbied the state fire marshall to try to get this enacted statewide. At that time, other states were using the one-key system, and we hoped Florida would also adopt it.

. . .

I had mentioned Larry Arthur as quite handsome, but we also had another crew member that was also handsome. His name was Jim Reynolds, and I'm happy to report that he, like his father, moved through the ranks and was eventually appointed to chief of the department.

One summer afternoon we responded to a fire on the eighth floor of the DuPont Centre, a twenty-eight-story high-rise building. As a crew we proceeded to the fire floor using one of the interior stairwells. I was a few paces behind Lieutenant Samillano, Larry, and Jim as they headed into the building. Lieutenant Samillano took the time to report to the command chief in the lobby before he started up, while Jim and Larry and I continued to the stairs and started the climb. I was about a half a flight or so behind them, favoring the right side of the stairwell, against the inside handrail. The building occupants who were evacuating downward stayed to their right, against the handrail attached to the masonry wall. Things were flowing well when three young ladies exiting together came in contact with Larry and Jim. As soon as the ladies passed them it was as if they were a drill team, reversing steps in unison and headed back up, staying close behind the two firefighters. They only took about three or four steps before once again reversing direction to continue downward. As they came by me, they were laughing and talking about how cute Larry and Jim were. They never saw me; they were too busy looking back toward them. As they passed, I smiled and continued upward.

Shortly afterwards we received a report from Engine Company 101's Lieutenant Tom Kelly saying no fire and they could handle it. We reversed our climb and headed back down. Back at the truck I shared with Jim and Larry what happened, and they weren't even aware. I laughed and told them it was entertaining.

. . .

When I was a child my mother and grandmother would take me downtown to shop. Back then, one of the tallest buildings was the Angebilt Hotel. It was built in the early 1920s and stood eleven stories. The top floor was a ballroom, and I remember my mother, my father, and my uncle Roy going to parties and dances at this once nice hotel. It had an elevator operator in each of the two elevators, and I was somewhat apprehensive when he would slide the folding scissor gate closed. As we ascended, I'd watch the closed hoist-way doors rapidly darting by through the gate.

One pleasant Saturday afternoon, February 27 of 1983, Firefighter Grant Aiello called me at my home to tell me he'd heard over his scanner that there was a fire at the Angebilt Hotel. Since we both lived close to downtown, he came by and picked me up. Moving quickly down Robinson Street, Grant turned onto Rosalind Avenue, heading to the firehouse. From my passenger window, I could see the north and east side of the hotel. Fire was roaring from two large top-floor windows on the north side of the building. I said to Grant that they got a good job. We quickly retrieved our fire helmets, coats, three-quarter rubber boots, and flashlights, and proceeded to the fire.

On arrival we met with Chief Chaney, the lobby commander, and he assigned Grant to assist with the fire attack. He asked me to make sure all hotel guests were evacuated from the tenth floor. He handed me a portable radio, and I donned an air pack from Engine 2, married together a Halligan bar and flat-headed axe, slung a rescue rope over my shoulder, and, in my right hand, carried two air cylinders by their tank valves. He said the elevators were inoperable and to take the south stairwell. Grant would take the north stairwell; this was the fire attack stairwell.

I started up the stairs and by the sixth floor I was getting quite tired, I decided to leave one air cylinder leaning in the corner of the stairwell and pushed upward. Reaching the tenth floor, I needed to rest, just to catch my breath. This was interrupted when Lieutenant Hullete came through the closed stairwell door out of air. He leaned over with his hands on his knees and rested while I unlatched the empty cylinder, turned off the tank valve, unscrewed the female inlet from the regulator, and slid the tank up and out of its harness. I would then replace it with the extra cylinder I brought with me. Once completed he went back to fighting the fire and I exited the stairwell to begin my search.

There was only a light haze of smoke on the floor, so I made quick work of entering the unlocked rooms. It appeared this entire floor wasn't rented out. At the time of the fire this once grand hotel had fallen into economic hardship and disrepair.

Grant and I had somewhat of an advantage because we knew this building quite well. We, along with Lieutenant Samillano made this our first pre-fire-plan building. We had read in a fire journal publication about this new idea or concept for gathering vital information for potentially dangerous fire buildings in your response area. We spent time in and around this building collecting information: the type of construction; the roof system; the location of the elevators and stairwells; the location of the standpipe connection, and the electrical and gas shutoffs, and more. We went to the planning department at city hall and got copies of the building's plans and layout. From this information the lieutenant drew an accurate floor plan of the lobby, top floor ballroom, and the floors in between. We also wrote down all vital information that would be useful if we had an emergency at this building. On Sunday afternoons, we'd capitalize on the light road traffic to position the tower ladder in different locations on the building for maximum reach and scrub area. This information gained was paying off now.

I reported to command an all clear for the tenth floor. I would proceed to the ballroom, the fire floor where I met up with Grant and numerous fire companies who were working frantically just to keep the fire from pushing them back and overrunning them. This top floor ballroom had high ceilings, approximately 12 feet high. The fire load was tremendous; it was filled from concrete floor to concrete ceiling with old mattresses, aging wooden beds, mirrors, lamps, toilets, and so forth.

Once again, the fire companies were doing what they were trained to do: "locate, confine, and extinguish." They had located the fire. It was confined, to some extent, because it was on the top floor, inside a concrete oven, so to speak. But there wasn't any way to ventilate the roof as it was poured concrete. Thankfully, the fact that it was a top-floor fire was a positive; although the flames were roaring out the north and west windows, it couldn't lap up the sides of the building and extend to upper floors. On the other hand, with the large open-floor plan, tightly packed heavy fire load, and the sheer size and intensity of the fire, the companies had a difficult time making progress.

A fire tactic that was considered and sometimes used was to move all firefighters back to the safety of the enclosed stairwell or floor below the fire and use exterior heavy caliber or large outside streams to knock down the fire. But before these streams were put in operation it was extremely important that all firefighters were off the fire floor. These powerful heavy streams can push fire and steam back into the building. Once the fire is knocked down the companies could move back in and, hopefully, extinguish the hidden pockets of fire.

The incident commander knew there was experienced aggressive company officers and seasoned crew members on the fire floor. He would rely on their evaluation of this stubborn fire. If they couldn't make any headway, they were professional enough to tell the commander, and he would change tactics.

Additional companies were arriving, working their way up the interior stairwell with hose slung over their shoulders and extra air cylinders. Multiple hose lines were now stretched to the fire floor off the standpipe system, which was located in the stairwell. This steel water pipe, 4 to 6 inches in diameter, extended from the ground floor or basement up and through the roof. At each floor there is a fire department hose connection to be used for fighting fires.

Engineer Art Maggio of Engine 101, hooked up to a fire hydrant and pumped water from the hydrant into the standpipe connection located on the outside of the building. This greatly increased the flow of water inside this pipe to accommodate the many hose lines. With fortitude and hard physical work these companies had started to make headway. We were able to advance deeper into the room knocking down fire. We spent hours fighting this challenging fire, but, in time and with a lot of hard work, we successfully extinguished it.

Once again, the firefighters and support personnel did a fine job. For me personally it felt good to be a member of the Orlando Fire Department and watching it grow into the profession it was meant to be.

· · ·

One Friday night, I was finishing up some kitchen duties. This involved straightening up the kitchen, washing remaining dishes, and mopping the tile floor. It was a little after 12:00 a.m. when I headed out to the dumpster carrying a plastic bag full of trash. The dumpster was 30 to 40 yards from the back door of the firehouse. It sat beside the rear driveway gate just outside the 8-foot-high chain-link fence. After depositing the trash, I then rolled the gate closed and locked it using a chain and padlock.

I raised the heavy steel lid just enough to pass the plastic bag between the lid and its 5-foot-high sides. In doing so, a female voice berated me with profanity as the trash bag came crashing down. But this profanity didn't have an angry sting to it. It appeared it was coming from someone who hadn't yet learned to use it in a mean or threatening way. I raised the lid more so a faint ray of light from a nearby streetlight could illuminate the inside of the dumpster. From this small amount of light, I saw the outline of a woman lying on the bags of trash. I told her how dangerous this was and that she should never seek refuge in a dumpster. While she stayed inside it, I asked her her age, was she homeless, and how she ended up in the dumpster, but she wouldn't say a word.

I continued with my concerns but the longer I was out there, the higher the probability that I could miss a call. I didn't want to leave her, but I needed my portable radio. I closed the lid and went to retrieve my radio. When I returned, she was still inside. I once again tried to convey the danger involved for a woman living on the street. But once again, she would not say a word. I shared with her that Doc, an alcoholic, who frequently slept behind the dumpster was due to arrive any time. Though I didn't think Doc wouldn't be a threat to her, I didn't tell her that. I only told her she could be in danger if he returned or with friends.

I shared with her my faith in God and wanted to sincerely convey my concern for her and that I wanted to help her. Still no response—not a word. I talked with her while she laid in the dumpster for close to thirty minutes. I believed she was listening. I finely convinced her to come out of the dumpster and sleep secured in the back of my pickup truck parked inside the fenced in area.

As I helped her out, I noticed her hair and face were clean. Her clothing looked fairly new, even fashionable. She had a generally healthy appearance. She just didn't fit the profile of the homeless I'd encountered on the streets of Orlando.

We walked through the gate opening, and I slid the gate closed and secured the lock. My truck was parked just inside the gate, and she climbed over the tailgate and inside. Once again, I tried to convince her to tell me her name and let me know how I could help her. By now it was close to 1:45 a.m., and I wasn't making any headway. I told her there wasn't any chance of rain, but it could get cool, and I would get her a blanket and pillow. I returned and she placed the pillow at the front of the truck's bed, laid down under the blanket, to hopefully sleep. I told her I would check back in the morning if I didn't get a call. I set my alarm clock earlier than normal and fell asleep.

Waking early, I walked to my truck, looked inside, and saw that she was asleep. I went back to the kitchen and fixed her a ham and egg sandwich. I found a few other food items and put them in a brown paper bag. When I returned to my truck it was starting to get light and she was waking up. I said hi and gave her the sandwich. She was hungry and ate it quickly.

Once again, I tried to get her to communicate with me but still no response. I wrote my name and telephone number of the firehouse on a piece of paper and gave it to her. I told her if she needed help, and I wasn't on duty to leave a message, I would get back to her. I folded the blanket and after she climbed down from the truck I gave it to her, telling her to keep it. I then open the rear gate and she walked through. I watched her leave with the blanket under her arm and the paper bag in her hand. It was March and that day's forecast was going to be sunny and mild. I continued to watch her walk through the small hedge that borders the firehouse and the FSI Building, through FSI's parking lot and then it was as if she just disappeared.

My heart was heavy for this young woman. I couldn't explain the late-night encounter nor what had just happened. I never heard from her again, nor did I see her in my remaining years with the department. I never called the police; in fact, it never came to mind. We had such a large homeless community in downtown Orlando, and they were a common site.

About twenty years after this incident, when I had already retired I was back in Orlando visiting my parents. It happened to be in March, and was meeting Joe Samillano for lunch. We decided since it was such a beautiful mild day, we would enjoy a "sloppy salami," our favorite sub sandwich at Momma B's restaurant at the corner of Orange Avenue and Colonial Drive. After lunch, we walked part of our old response area, our old turf, reminiscing fires and emergencies. Walking west on Church Street in front of the SunTrust Bank Building and I saw a woman in her thirties holding a sign that read "homeless." I stopped directly in front of her and read her neatly written sign. She was wearing a pair of clean black slacks and white long sleeve sweater. Her face and hair were clean, and she had a healthy appearance. As I stared into her face, she stared back with knowing eyes. A strange feeling came over me. I told her I was sorry she was homeless, and Joe and I reached into our pockets and handed her some money. She reached out and excepted the money but said nothing. I stood for a moment taking in what was happening, then we turned and walked over the railroad tracks and stepped inside the Cheyenne Saloon & Opera House. Joe ordered us a pitcher of beer, and we decided to enjoy it at a sidewalk table. I stepped outside and looked back toward the SunTrust Bank building, but she was gone, like she had disappeared.

I couldn't help but wonder if this was the same woman. Joe and I enjoyed the beer and conversation, but this young lady was in the back of my mind. When we left and walked east on Church Street my eyes searched the street and surrounding area, but I didn't see her.

I'm now in my seventies, and it's been thirty-five years since my first encounter with the young woman. I believe the woman that Joe and I saw on Church Street was the same person. These thirty-five years I've wondered and tried to make sense of those two meetings. I don't believe it was a coincidence. I've had experiences in the past that I believe were spiritual but there wasn't anything spiritual with the encounter with this woman—or if there was, I couldn't and still can't see it. I would like to know what it is, especially if it's to impact my life or someone else's. But up until now the only impact I'm feeling is a sadness for another human being. Though that is something of value, to feel compassion and caring for a fellow human being. I can't, however, see any value that came from the meetings with that young woman.

• • •

I've mentioned Doc, the alcoholic, who slept behind our dumpster. Sometimes when returning from a run late at night Doc, we'd find him passed out in the middle of the driveway. We would stop the truck, and two crew members would pick him up and carry him to his cardboard bed. Sometimes late at night, when I went to deposit trash, Doc would be lying on his well-worn cardboard. If he wasn't so intoxicated that he was passed out, I would share my hope in God and my concerns for him. Sometimes we had meaningful conversations, but I was aware some homeless folks will tell you what they think you want to hear to get something from you. I felt Doc wasn't like that, however.

Other firefighters got to know him and also befriended him. One firefighter-paramedic was Rob Mitchell. Rob was one of those individuals who would literally give you the shirt off his back. I felt Rob may have had to deal with alcoholism in his family, he knew the destructive nature alcohol can produce.

He took Doc under his wing. He took Doc to Alcoholic Anonymous meetings, cleaned him up, bought him new clothing, and rented him a room in a house behind the firehouse. One pleasant winter day, I was standing outside the back door of the firehouse and noticed a man walk through the open driveway gate. At that distance, I didn't recognize who it was. As he got closer, I noticed he had on a new colorful red-and-white flannel shirt, new jeans, a belt, and leather shoes. It also looked like he had just bathed and shaved. I still didn't recognize this man until he said, "Bill, it's Doc." I couldn't believe the transformation. I hadn't seen him in a while and thought he had just moved on, or something tragic happened to him. He told me that Rob made this possible, he had even found him a job as a janitor. One afternoon I saw Rob and Doc sitting on the park bench outside the back door of the firehouse in meaningful conversation. I was moved by both of them and hoped it would continue.

Though I'm sorry to say, Doc was unable to continue in this new lifestyle and went back and embraced the bottle. One Saturday morning, our work shift had just begun, Rescue 1 was dispatched to a cutting underneath the East-West Expressway at Rosalind Street. The victim, I'm sad to say, was Doc, who was dead due to knife wounds. He was lying only fifty yards from his old, abandoned, cardboard bed behind the dumpster.

. . .

For a brief period, we had an arsonist setting fires to downtown buildings. A young man was finally arrested but not after setting a string of fires. The fires I personally went to were all in vacant buildings a few blocks north of downtown and all were started with materials found on site; no flammable liquids were used. The news media called this person "the downtown arsonist." He seemed to strike on the weekends, after midnight. During this time, if our communications section announced that "everyone goes," we were fairly certain we were going to a fire. One such fire was in a large old factory building at the corner of Marks Street and Orange Avenue. After quickly rolling out of bed, I slid the pole to the apparatus floor, jumped into the driver's seat of the tower ladder, and one by one, each apparatus took their turn leaving the station, heading north on Magnolia Avenue. The once full apparatus floor now had an eerie emptiness with work shoes scattered across the reddish-brown ceramic tile floor.

When responding to these fires, we could often smell the distinct odor of a structure fire. But tonight, as we got close to the address, we still couldn't see or smell anything. But once we turned left onto Marks Street, we knew we had a good working fire ahead of us.

I'm not sure of the age of this heavy timber-frame constructed building with thick masonry brick walls. Likely it was the equivalent of a three-story building but with only two floors. Built before air conditioning, it had large, steel, heavy, wired-glass factory windows that were hinged at the midpoint so they could be pivoted open—the bottom of the windows would shift outside the building and the top of the windows would shift to the inside. This was a fairly good design at that time; it not only allowed for maximum air flow and light, but when rainstorms came, they could be left open (unless it was a blowing rain). Because the windows had been installed quite high on the walls, the top inside portion that extended inside the room wasn't an obstruction, or a "head knocker". The large solidly built wooden floors were strong enough to support numerous 1950s and '60s automobiles that were much heavier than today's automobiles. It had a ramp for the automobile dealership next door, off Marks Street, so the cars could be driven up to the second floor for storage. I don't think the original building was built for car storage. I do remember that it had also been a furniture factory at one time.

Just a week before the fire, we had walked through that same building. It wasn't locked, and the windows were wide open, a prime target for the arsonist. Plus, there was plenty of scrap wood and sawdust for building a fire. Additionally, the floors were oil-soaked from the automobiles, which could undoubtedly add to the intensity of the fire. We commented on what a huge fire this building could produce, not knowing that the following Saturday night we would be back.

Heading west on Marks Street we spotted a large open parking lot on the east side of the building. Lieutenant Joe Samillano felt this would be the best spot for our apparatus. I pulled into the parking lot and drove north just past the large factory windows roaring fire. We had a good spot on the building to possibly stop the fire from moving northward, but we needed a good water supply to give it a try. Lieutenant Joe stepped down and said, "I'm going to try to get you water." I exited the driver's seat, and, once outside the truck, I encountered the sheer noise of this fire roaring from the windows. It hadn't broken through the roof, so this confined fire under a lot of pressure sought out the large open windows. The heavy fire exited the windows like a blowtorch, extending far out into the parking lot then bending skyward. The noise was deafening. I had to yell so Firefighter Larry Arthur could hear me standing beside him. We would wait until supply lines were heading our way to set the truck up, I told him. I had a gut feeling, we were positioned just past the fire and there was no incident commander in that area, somewhat "out of sight, out of mind," the water supply lines would be stretched to the front of the building where more equipment had congregated. I only took the time to set the air brake and engage the PTO (power take-off) to operate the outrigger jacks. I extended both left and right midship jacks located just under the turntable outwards but didn't lower them. If we got water, Larry would position the ground support pads under the jacks on the right side of the truck, and I would take care of the ones on the left. It soon became apparent we weren't going to get one of the first water supply lines. The fire was moving our way, and the radiant heat was starting to melt the bucket and side marker lights. Larry and I decided to move the truck farther down the building, hoping we would get water soon. By the time we got water, the fire advanced to the end of the building and our thoughts about beating it back or holding it to only part of the building was not to be. Tower ladders were set up, and ground monitors positioned around the building poured water for hours into this now crumbling structure. It was doubtful we could have stopped such a heavy volume of fire, but it would have been interesting to find out. For historic sake, to lose such an old well-built building was a shame. I wonder if the arsonist was watching the fire and our actions.

. . .

One other fire this arsonist set was quite memorable for me. It wasn't a roaring blaze, nor spectacular in appearance. It wasn't about the actual building fire but more about the fire companies, and how they operated as an orchestra at this fire.

When I attended Fern Creek Elementary school in the 1950s, we would be bused along with every other elementary school in Orange County to the Bob Carr Auditorium to hear the Florida Symphony Orchestra. I wasn't keen on classical music, but when they played the "William Tell Overture," recognizing it as the theme music from the *Lone Ranger*, the packed auditorium came alive with cheers. To listen to a full orchestra is quite moving for me. I love seeing the variety of professional talented musicians come together to produce a beautiful piece of work. This is what I would experience tonight, each fire company contributing their expertise to produce a well-orchestrated and successful operation.

Once again, the alarm was transmitted after midnight on the weekend. The address of the fire was in the 600 block of North Orange Avenue across the street from the *Orlando Sentinel* newspaper. As we headed north on Magnolia Avenue, I said to Joe that there was nothing there, meaning most of that block. The west side of Orange Avenue had been cleared of structures due to a recent fire in a motel. When we got to East Amelia Street, we began to smell the fire, so we knew we had something. Turning left onto East Concord Street, we passed the newspaper building on our right and stopped at the intersection of Concord Street and Orange Avenue. Engine 1, under the command of Lieutenant Charlie Menchen, took a right onto Orange Avenue to investigate. We waited at the intersection while Engine 1 scanned the area. I said to Joe, "I think it's farther south." Chief Steve Carter, the commander, asked us over the radio to investigate down the street. We turned left and went almost two blocks when we came upon the building. The doors and windows had been boarded up with sheets of plywood. Smoke was seeping out from between the plywood sheets and the frames around these openings. The building was one story of a brick and wood joist construction, approximately 100' x 100'.

Lieutenant Joe Samillano reported to command what we'd found, and I started positioning the truck on the building. I was quite pleased because I had four open lanes of roadway to maneuver. There were no obstacles such as overhead power lines, telephone poles, or other fire trucks to contend with.

I pulled the truck parallel to the middle of the building about 30 feet away for good scrub area. I also move the truck's cab about 15 degrees away from the building so the cab wouldn't obstruct the aerial boom if having to operate toward the front of the truck. I was now in an ideal position for aerial operations.

Chief Carter, a most respected and competent commander, requested an additional engine and ladder company to respond. Firefighter Denny Longest, OVM, who was detailed from Ladder 11, set the outrigger support pads on the right side of the truck, and I set the left. We had trained to be proficient at setting up our apparatus. By the time the air brake was engaged we could have the bucket ready for operation within one minute.

In a rescue situation, this was a fast time to have the truck stable, secure, and moving into position for rescue of occupants. Though on this night occupant rescue wasn't a concern, we still moved quickly wanting to get to the roof.

With the structure boarded up, Lieutenant Samillano had his forcible entry firefighter secure one of the K12 power saw's. Firefighter Longest grabbed the other saw, then hung it from a hook attached to the outside of the bucket and climbed in. Lastly, before I climbed in, I turned on the generator that powered the large quartz lights to the truck and bucket. By now, Engine 101 was on the scene and Lieutenant Tom Kelly had Firefighter Reggie Pride pull a 1¾-inch hose line to the front door. Engineer Dave Baldino, always thinking, hand laid a 4-inch supply line to the fire hydrant across the street. Lifting the bucket out of the cradle, heading to the roof, I could see all personnel doing what they do best. Hose was being charged, straightened for entry, and bled of air. Engineer Baldino was at the pump panel increasing pressure to the hand line. The forcible entry firefighter was cutting an opening in the plywood sheeting covering the entry door (we referred to this as cutting a door within a door). Chief Carter was overseeing all operations. All personnel were engaged in their duties or assignments. Once again, I could see a close professional team working together for a common cause. I had been a team player all my life and to see my fellow teammates flow was inspiring.

As I got closer to the roof, I noticed the parapet was only about 3 feet high. I decided to lift the bucket over this parapet wall and set the bucket on the roof. Firefighter Longest would exit the bucket and make his way to the remaining three walls, looking over to see if any fire, smoke or occupants were at any windows or anything unusual to report. I would make a quick size up.

The roof was considered flat, with a slight pitch for rain to run off from front to rear. The construction was full 2x12 wood joists, placed on 16-inch centers with 1x6 boards laid at a 45-degree angle to the joists. The covering was rolled roofing with tarred seams. There were twelve to sixteen turbine ventilators equally spaced on the roof, and all had smoke coming from them. The ones at the front of the building were emitting more smoke than the ones at the rear. The two directly in front of the bucket were emitting the most smoke, and I could see they were under some pressure. I reported to Chief Carter that I was going to make an opening about 20 feet in from the front of the building, directly in line with the bucket. As I started the saw and began the cut, Firefighter Jim Reynolds came up the aerial boom ladder to help with the opening. The power saw cut the roof extremely easy, and Denny and Jim used their Halligan hooks to remove the sheeting and roofing material. Using their hooks, they pushed the ceiling down and in doing so could see the fire below. The smoke went from black to light gray, so it was clear the water had reached the seat of the fire. I heard over my radio, "Fire knocked down." We checked the cockloft to make sure the fire hadn't made its way inside.

Lieutenant Samillano asked us to report to him when we had completed our tasks. We finished up, gathered all equipment, and headed down. Once on the ground, we met with Lieutenant Samillano and he took us inside to the fire location. Inside, I could see why he and the chiefs had a smile on their face. Our ventilation opening was directly over the fire, and when Denny and Jim pushed the ceiling down it literally landed on top of the arsonist fire. Once again this wasn't a major fire, but everyone on the scene was pleased about how smooth it went. All companies and commanders knew what was expected of them and performed them superbly. This was a textbook operation, and I was pleased and honored to not only experience such an operation but to also experience the thrill of working beside my brothers and sisters, who I truly respect.

. . .

I had once read that to be directly over the fire could be very dangerous, which I agreed with. It went on to say the roof team should be as close over the fire as was safe. That always made perfect sense, though I did position myself over a well-established fire and came close to falling through the roof. The fire came in on a gray midmorning on Thanksgiving Day. We had already started cooking the thanksgiving meal when companies from our firehouse and Station 2 were dispatched to the Quarterback Club on South Street just west of Division Avenue.

We would be the second due ladder company this cool misty morning. The fire was reported in the rear, or stock room area, of this one-story open-for-business bar. Tower Ladder 2, first to arrive, positioned their truck in front of the building that faced South Street. Engine 2 positioned its apparatus behind the tower ladder just east of the building, a good position from which to pull attack hose lines to the stockroom door opening at the exterior of the building. Engine 1 brought in a large diameter water supply line and connected it to Engine 2. Crews from both Engine 1 and 101 pulled additional hand lines from Engine 2 and pulled them to the exterior door.

We positioned Tower Ladder 1 just past Tower Ladder 2, if needed, to operate on the west, or left, side of the building. Tower Ladder 2's bucket had transported its roof team to the roof to size up the situation. Grant and I each secured a power saw and climbed Tower Ladder 2's aluminum ladder affixed to the top of its boom. The lieutenant and rest of our crew grabbed additional Halligan hooks and proceeded to the storeroom. Grant and I experienced great difficulty climbing this extremely low angle ladder—it was extremely slippery from the misty rain and a thin coating of hydraulic oil. Because the ladder was at such a low angle, we weren't able to sling the saws over our shoulder to keep both hands free. We were carrying a cumbersome 35-pound saw in one hand and holding onto the low handrail with the other, plus our rubber three-quarter boots were slipping and sliding on each rung.

Once on the roof I heard Lieutenant Dick Schuren of Engine 2 over my portable radio requesting roof ventilation, as there wasn't any openings for horizontal ventilation except for the one door they entered. As the companies moved deeper into the storeroom, the ladder companies were having great difficulty making an opening in the ceiling to check for fire over their heads. It was determined the ceiling was made up of 1x6 tongue and groove boards. With the heat building the incident commander asked us how our roof ventilation was going. The ladder company was having trouble starting their saw. Noticing this, I immediately started my saw and began to cut open the roof. Making my first cut perpendicular to the roof joists, I could see fire through the kerf opening made by the circular saw blade. Because it was such a dark gray day, it resembled a straight orange line on the roof. As I turned the saw ninety degrees to cut in between the joists, the roof settled, and this once thin straight line of fire became an inch wide. I knew I was in a dangerous area and quickly moved to safety toward the front of the fire building.

Upon reporting our situation to the chief in command he asked if we could try again as close to the fire as was safe. By now Grant had his saw running, and we started another opening in a safer location but still close to the origin of the fire. A firefighter from Tower Ladder 2 got their saw running, so now we had three saws operating. Things were flowing nicely until the wind changed direction. For a moment we were enveloped in smoke and lost all visibility, which was unnerving, knowing three power saws with their exposed sharp carbide tip blades were spinning at great speeds. Luckily the wind shifted again but not after a few long seconds of fright. By now the fire had control of the attic space at the back of the building. It was venting out a cockloft ventilation vent at the top of the north wall. The fire was also breaking through the failed roof opening I had started. The interior ladder companies weren't making any headway getting the ceiling pulled down to get water into the cockloft. They had managed to get a few small openings, but the engine companies' streams didn't have the volume of water necessary to knock down such a large volume of fire.

The commander in charge, Chief Alan MacAllaster, didn't like what he was seeing and decided to pull everyone out of the building and off the roof. He had the crew of Tower Ladder 1 reposition their apparatus to the north side of the building to operate a heavy caliber bucket stream into the cockloft ventilation opening at the top of its wall. This tactic worked, and this heavy volume of water extinguished the fire in the cockloft. Once it was knocked down and it was determined it was safe, the crews reentered the structure to extinguish any smaller fires.

It was a stubborn, challenging fire, but once again, all companies performed professionally and aggressively. With everything now under control, the commander released a few companies to return to quarters. The apparatus I was on was one of those companies. I was in the storeroom preforming overhaul when I heard over my portable radio Lieutenant Samillano telling us to "take up," meaning collect all tools and report back to the apparatus. I decided to walk through the door separating the storeroom from the main bar area. It was satisfying to see that the firefighting companies were able to keep the fire from this area. Everything looked fine; even the lights above the bar were on. I thought this was somewhat strange since we usually cut the electrical power to the building on arrival. I don't know what made me do this, as I wasn't a huge fan of beer, but I walked behind the bar, grabbed a cold glass mug, and stood in front of four draft beer tap handles. I don't remember the beer I selected, but I filled my glass half full—I didn't want a buzz, only a cold refreshing drink. I knew drinking alcohol on the job wasn't allowed, but a small swig wouldn't be that bad. All these years later, I understand the dangers of alcohol. A cold beer can bring comfort and peace in certain situations, but if abused, it can bring destruction.

. . .

To take one's own life is something I can't fully understand. As I've grown older and experienced more of life, I've grown to understand it somewhat better. On a scale from one to ten—one being "I'd never take my life" and ten "I might attempt to take it," I predict we all fall somewhere on this scale. That some folks find themselves at the upper end of this scale is heart wrenching for me, yet I can somewhat understand. I was on calls where someone had taken their life. Most firefighters experience this sometime in their career.

We responded one late night to just such a call, to a house fire just off Bumby Avenue. There was little traffic at 2:00 a.m., so it was easy access to the East-West expressway. We arrived on the scene a few seconds after Engine 6 and Rescue 6. The structure was located in the middle of the block and the scene was quite dark: the only streetlights were at the intersections, and the front of the house was obscured by water oak trees. The quartz lights from the apparatus did little to light the area. Even with our flashlight at hand, there were plenty of trip hazards to deal with. It appeared the fire was at the back of the one-story, wood-frame, single-family dwelling. Engine 6 pulled one 1¾-inch hose line to the front door. Lieutenant Joe Samillano, Gerry Kasper (the forcible entry man), and the crew from Rescue 6 also entered through this front door. I secured my 6-foot Halligan hook and 30-inch Halligan bar, married them together, and went around to the back of the structure. I discovered a fire just inside the enclosed back porch.

Engine 4, the second due engine company, brought in a water supply line from the fire hydrant just down the street. Patty Donahue, off of Engine 4, was directed to pull another 1¾-inch hose line down the driveway next to the house to the rear of the structure. Patty and I went through this back door. She knocked down fire while I started a search. We came upon an open metal military ammunition can filled to the top with handgun ammunition. I recognize the container as it was the same size and shape that M60 machine gun ammunition came in. Due to the heat produced from the fire, the rounds were "cooking off," so Patty quickly maneuvered the hose line and filled the can with water. (I've encountered rounds "cooking off" when I was in Vietnam. Our machine gun barrels and receivers could get extremely hot from firing countless rounds, without stopping to let them cool. So even if the trigger wasn't pulled, this extreme heat could ignite the gun powder in the cartridge that's seated in the chamber, sending the bullet out the end of the barrel.) Since the bullets in the open ammunition box we'd found weren't chambered inside a gun, they likely weren't overly dangerous. They might split out the side of the cartridge brass casing and produce a popping noise. Even so, there's always a concern when dealing with ammunition, and Patty quickly responded to the situation.

We encountered numerous rifles, pistols and ammunition on our search. Lieutenant Samillano and Gerry found the victim fully dressed lying on his back on top of a bed. Rigor mortis had set in, telling us he had been dead for at least a few hours, maybe more. He looked to be about my age, in his forties.

Engine 6 encountered another fire at the middle of the house and extinguished it. As the smoke began to clear, we noticed plastic bleach bottles filled with gasoline hanging from different locations inside the house and in the attic. Just a few inches beneath some of the bottles was a hot plate connected to a timer. We also noticed a pickup truck backed up against the exterior wall of the deceased's bedroom. A flexible hose was attached to the tailpipe of the truck, and the other end went through an opening in the house siding and extended into the bedroom. The truck wasn't running, the ignition was in the on position, and the gas gauge read empty. The entire house was damaged due to the fires—all except the deceased's bedroom. It appeared to me his plan was to take his life from carbon monoxide poisoning through the truck's exhaust, then burn the house and all his furnishings down around him. From what I saw, he was a military veteran.

We had no idea what we were crawling into. We were just fortunate we arrived in time to extinguish the fires and not have any gasoline-filled bleach bottles rain down upon us. I don't know if these bleach bottles were intended to burn down his house or a booby trap for firefighters. I also wonder if one of the two fires caused the electrical breakers to be thrown, thus cutting electrical power to the other hot plates.

I now wonder about this veteran and Larry, my high school buddy, and what caused them to get to the point of taking their lives. Luckily no one on the team was physically injured at that fire, but has it caused mental injuries to some of the firefighters.

· · ·

You just never know what you may encounter as a firefighter. I always liked that about the job, every emergency call is different in one way or another. So when the downtown arsonist struck again, we headed out the door heading north and a right on to Amelia Street. Engine 101 was leading the procession with the tower ladder behind them. We had to stop around Geneva Place due to a quite tall and wide wooden street barrier placed across the street. It also had flashing lights affixed to its top. On the middle horizontal board was a large sign, haphazardly attached, with the words ROAD CLOSED. It was more of a permanent barrier, yet quite flimsy than the usual light-duty low sawhorse-type barrier. We could see the structure fire about a half block up the street lighting up the area. Firefighter Reggie Pride jumped off Engine 101 and started to pull this large barrier from the roadway so we could proceed. From the windshield, Lieutenant Samillano and I watched Reggie, then up the street to the fire, then back at Reggie, then back at the fire. Reggie was doing his best to move the cumbersome barrier, then, all of a sudden, the entire unit came apart and collapsed on top of him. We started to laugh. Reggie wasn't hurt, only entwined in the numerous red wooden boards and flashing lights. Seeing Reggie wasn't injured and able to extricate himself, Engine

101 left him and proceeded down the torn-up dirt street to the fire. I also accelerated and waved to Reggie as we went by. I'm not sure if anyone stopped to give him a ride, maybe the chief, but he may have had to walk the half block. We all got a good laugh, even Reggie. Though we did get an earful later, he had a way with words—we loved him.

Arriving in front of the boarded-up wood-frame house, the fire appeared to have complete control of the entire structure. If I remember correctly, the arsonist set the fire in the open crawl space under the house. We pulled numerous hand lines to protect the two exposed houses on either side of the fire about 12 feet away. After knocking down the fire and determining it was safe to enter, we went inside and started our overhaul. Engineer-paramedic Dewey Speegle from Rescue 1 fell through the floor where the fire started and injured his leg. He was transported to the hospital with minor injuries. I believe Dewey was the only firefighter injured by the reign of the downtown arsonist.

. . .

There were those buildings or street addresses that fire companies would frequently respond to. In some company's first due response area they may respond to this same address at least once or maybe more during a twenty-four-hour shift. We had such an address at the intersection of Anderson Street and Mills Avenue. All companies at Firehouse 1 had responded to this address numerous times. The structure was a small one-story, concrete-block duplex apartment. The residents in the apartment that faced Anderson Street was a mother and daughter. The mother worked during the day and her twenty-year-old daughter was mostly confined to a wheelchair, sadly dying of HIV/AIDS. The times our apparatus responded to this young woman we were usually met with anger and bitterness. She was deeply troubled, and I'm quite certain this deadly virus was taking a toll on her mind. It was easy to see she was once attractive and possibly had a fulfilling life, but now she was extremely thin, disheveled, mean, and belligerent.

One afternoon we received a call to assist her back into her wheelchair. Lieutenant Mike Lojko happened to be our company officer that day. We entered through the unlocked carport door because the front door was always locked and usually had a large heavy sofa slid in front of it. That afternoon she was lying on the floor in the living room next to her chair. We picked her up and sat her back into her chair. As I stood beside her, listening to Lieutenant Mike and the young lady, I was struck by the compassionate caring tone of Lieutenant Mike and, in contrast, how hostile the tone of this young lady. I can't speak for other firefighters who had interacted with this woman, but this afternoon I witnessed a kind compassionate firefighter, conveying from his heart, a nonjudgmental deep concern for a fellow human being. Mike nor I knew how she had gotten into this predicament, but she was treated with kindness and respect.

One cool sunny morning around 8:00, we were in the process of checking over the apparatus, making sure they and all equipment were ready for another twenty-four-hour shift. Our apparatus happened to be one firefighter short, the firefighter occupying the jump seat behind me. We were still in service and available for calls but waiting for a detailed firefighter to arrive from another firehouse.

Once again, those attention-getting, adrenaline-pumping words, EVERYONE GOES, made its way to all ears in and around the firehouse. With many of the firefighters at their apparatus this would decrease our response time. The address was in the 1100 block of East Anderson Street, we knew it well. At that time in the morning most traffic was coming into the city, not leaving, so Anderson Street wasn't going to be packed with automobiles as it would be at 5:00 p.m. Our response time would last only minutes.

Engine Company 1 would lead out with the tower ladder behind them, then Engine Company 101 and the chief in command bringing up the rear. Rescue Company 1 was responding from south of town and would arrive last.

Engine 1 pulled just past the address, so the lieutenant could see three sides of the structure, helping with size up. We pulled up and stopped behind them, and I set the emergency air brakes. On the south side of the street, fire was pushing out of one living room window in this small quite familiar duplex apartment. Engine 1 pulled one 1¾-inch attack hose line and started stretching it to the front door. Lieutenant Samillano and his forcible entry man would force this door. Engine 101 pulled up to the hydrant waiting for word to bring in a water supply line. I immediately foresaw how this was playing out and knew what was expected of me. With one crew member short, I alone would most likely be the person to locate the young woman and possibly her mother. But I felt the mother may not have been home because her car wasn't parked in the carport.

Quickly donning my air pack and securing my tools I headed to the carport. As I got closer, I could hear the distinct sound of the flat headed axe striking the Halligan forcible entry bar. This sharp distinct sound let Chief Steve Carter know forcible entry was in process. I would enter through the door from the carport into their small kitchen.

This half glass, nine lite, wooden door was locked. Seeing no deadbolt lock I simply had to use the adze end of the Halligan bar to break out one small windowpane next to the doorknob, reach through, and turn the knob. Once inside the small kitchen I could visually search this area. The smoke was dense at the ceiling, yet became somewhat transparent as it moved downward; it was quite toxic, however, and I knew I would need my mask. I had thought I may not need to take the time to don it, saving a few valuable seconds, that I would find her unconscious in the living room, either in her wheelchair or on the living room floor, scoop her up, and take her out through the kitchen carport door. But whatever was burning I knew it was dangerously harmful, and without my mask I may also be a victim.

I quickly proceeded into the living room, the fire room. To my left was only blackness, and upward at the ceiling was the reddish orange glow making its dance across the ceiling. All interior firefighters have witnessed this phenomenon. It wasn't too hot, maybe because it was venting out the front windows. I no longer heard the Halligan and axe but did hear someone say, "The door's blocked." It didn't dawn on me that it was probably the sofa. I was too intent on finding the woman or the wheelchair. I moved as close to the fire as possible and blindly searched, extending my legs and arms in a sweeping pattern—the area was all clear. As I looked to my right, I could make out the back wall of the living room. Coming in contact with the opposite living room wall, I moved to my right, toward the hallway.

There were now only two rooms and a short hallway to search. I looked right as I crawled into the hallway and could see to its end; she wasn't there. Immediately to my left was the bedroom with its door open. The dense smoke was banked about a third of the way from the ceiling, but below that I had good visibility. Staying low I search the bed, under the bed, the floor area next to it, and a small closet. As I completed the search Firefighter-Paramedic Frank Cornier from Rescue 1, was squeezing through a small casement window. That was quite a feat through such a narrow opening, but he made it. Frank said to me, "Did you find her?"

"No," I said, "she must be in the bathroom." I thought to myself, if she's in the bathroom we may have a difficult time removing her. And if she's unconscious on the floor between the tub and toilet and her wheelchair is between us this would be even more difficult. The longer she's inside this toxic environment the shorter her chance of survival.

I quickly moved down the hall, then a right into the bathroom, but she wasn't there either. I reported to Frank that she wasn't in the bathroom, and he immediately started a secondary search. I knew I had made a good search; I knew the layout of the apartment, and the smoke conditions weren't that bad. I just felt I couldn't have missed her. The engine and ladder company had pushed the door enough to get inside and knocked down the fire. I quickly moved to the fire location; the heavy sofa had been pushed away from the wall by the forced open front door. On the sofa lay the burnt body of the young lady. Next to the sofa sat her charred wheelchair, a stark reality of the tragedy.

As the smoke continued to lift and exit the broken front windows I saw Jay Griner, the driver of Engine 1, standing just outside the window. Our eyes met, our faces solemn.

. . .

In the summer of 1995, for reasons I can't explain, I began to feel a strangeness toward my fire department career. Up until this time, I considered myself enthusiastic, and some of my coworkers would have said I was gung-ho. I loved the challenges of our profession; I always looked forward to coming to work. I had often said that I loved the profession so much I didn't feel like I would ever retire. I thought I'd work in combat as long as I was physically able, then move to a day job in a different section of the department. That way I would still be involved with the department and able to contribute to it and to the citizens of Orlando.

But now something was happening within me. My enthusiasm was slowly waning. I felt I was being pulled to pursue another career, or maybe an adventure of some sort. I talked with my wife about my feelings and retirement. We both had become disappointed in how the city was growing, the concrete, traffic, crime, and noise.

Jeanne, my wife, had grown up in rural Tennessee and we had visited that area often. I did like the slower pace, small town appeal, and fewer automobiles. It also had four seasons, with cooler temperatures. I liked the rolling hills and streams of the countryside, varieties of different hardwoods, and the sheer beauty of the area.

We decided I would retire after I completed my twenty-fifth year, and then we'd move to Tennessee. I continued to give 100 percent to my admirable profession. Friday, my last day on shift, I was assigned to the entry-man position for hazardous materials calls. That morning, we responded to a natural gas leak on, I think, Washington Street just west of Interstate 4. On arrival we were informed a backhoe had broken an underground gas line. My backup firefighter and I changed into our bright yellow jumpsuits with HAZ MAT written on the back. We called them banana suits because of their color. I seem to recall they were made of some type of fire-retardant material, similar to my Nomex flight suit.

Now, dressed in the jumpsuit, Lieutenant Joe Samillano walked up to tell me I wasn't going to lead the entry team. He said this being my last day the commander decided to replace me with another firefighter. I balked at this decision and voiced my protest. For me, personally, if something was going to happen, I should have to deal with it and not someone else just because it was my last day on duty. If something tragic happened to the person who took my place, I would feel terrible. But it turned out the gas company had also arrived on the scene. They were able to locate a shutoff valve and stop the flow of gas.

The rest of the shift was uneventful with a few photographs taken after the evening meal. The next morning, I was relieved by the engineer of B shift. I walked down the narrow hallway to the back door, crossed over the threshold, and never looked back. That same day Jeanne and I and our yellow lab, Scout, piled into the front seat of our pickup truck and hit the road to Tennessee.

Moving Forward

Tennessee was a welcome change from Florida. Though it was the summer of 1996, Tennessee, seemed to me, not near as hot as Orlando. I found this very refreshing because I knew I would be working outdoors the rest of the summer months and into the fall. My wife and I had purchased some acreage on which to build our home, and my first duties would be to clear the building site, which was heavily forested. A lot of the trees were quite tall and very large at their base. I was somewhat intimidated by their size. I found a local logger who was interested in the trees—which were maple, red and white oaks, hickory, and poplar . . . all nice hardwoods—and would pay me for them. I thought it was a good deal for both of us.

When Mr. Brown showed up early one morning, I wasn't prepared to meet a gentleman almost twenty years older than I was. He was, however, quite fit, and well-mannered in a humble way. We hit it off immediately. One of his first questions after our introduction was if I had a church yet. He told me if I didn't, he'd like to invite me to his. I found out quite quickly this question was asked of every new person who moved to the buckle of the Bible Belt. It would be asked many times over the next year.

He selected the trees that he felt were worth taking. I had marked a large circle around the perimeter where the house would sit. Everything outside of that perimeter was not to be cut. I would be his helper. He would fell the trees, and I would help with limbing, and hook a chain to the log. Mr. Brown brought his blue New Holland tractor and would drag the log about 600 feet down a logging road that we would also use as a driveway to the street. Some of these logs were almost 30 feet long. We worked well together; he was a hard methodical worker, a thing I respected given my work history. He rarely got a fallen tree hung up in other standing trees, and if he did, he knew exactly how to get it the rest of the way down. These massive trees were over my head, so to speak, and I was fortunate to have Mr. Brown's expertise.

When we took our break for lunch—Mr. Brown called it "the dinner meal"—we sat on a downed log under the canopy of one of my maple trees. Even at noon in my new Tennessee environment, the mild temperatures were a welcoming relief from the hot humid summers of Orlando. For dinner, Mr. Brown unwrapped from a small sheet of waxed paper a bologna sandwich on white bread. I was having a tomato sandwich with some cut-up cantaloupe and watermelon. We ended up having nice conversations about logging and the Flynns Lick community where he grew up.

It took us about three days to fell his trees, but there were still some larger trees he couldn't use that stood scary tall, reaching high into the blue sky. I mentioned this to him, and he was happy to cut them for me, making my work much safer.

With his trees at the bottom of our driveway, he cut them into sawmill lengths and loaded them onto his logging truck. He was a one-man show with many years in this hard rugged business. He was doing what he loved as I was when I worked with the fire department, yet it was so different in many ways. I didn't know it at the time, but I was starting a new education, learning and understanding my new community and folks who inhabited it.

. . .

We still had a couple of months of major yardwork ahead of us: a lot of firewood to cut, and brush to drag into piles and burn, though I didn't like the prospect of burning. Initially, I had thought of dragging the smaller limbs and tops of trees to the outside of the circle and letting them decompose on their own. I ended up having a wall of brush about 5 feet high, and almost the entire circumference of the circle. I decided to drag the limbs back into the 200-foot diameter circle and burn them. Fall would be coming on, and I wanted to enjoy the foliage and not a lot of dead leaves. I had some time to burn before Mr. Dyer, a backhoe operator, arrived.

I was told he was the best in the Upper Cumberland, and after seeing him operate his machine, I could understand why he had that reputation. He was also known to have a beautiful singing voice. Apparently, folks came to his church just to hear him sing. He always wore a baseball hat and sang church songs when operating his machine. Mr. Dyer dug two separate trenches about 600 feet long and 3 feet deep. One was for the water line and the other for the electrical and telephone line. I installed the water line; the power and telephone company would lay theirs in their separate trench. At 11:30 that morning, the power company left for the "dinner meal," but Mr. Dyer sat on his backhoe trailer to eat his sandwich. I remember it was ham and cheese, not bologna, and he had Chip Ahoy chocolate chip cookies for dessert. I joined him with my to-mato sandwich, and he kindly shared his package of cookies. We talked about church, and I learned about the Dyers' who were well respected in the local community. Mr. Dyer also helped with the driveway, clearing a nice gentle path that meandered through the woods. He also called for a couple loads of rock to be spread on the driveway.

We continued to saw firewood, stacking the cords neatly. I was also burning brush, which made for a hot and dirty workday. With water now run to the property I filled five 1-gallon milk jugs with water and set them out in the sun to warm during the day. I remembered that when I was in Vietnam, the sun would warm the water tank and a warm shower felt so nice after a dirty sticky day of flying. In the late afternoon, I'd remove my clothes, stand on a pallet, and pour the warm water over my head to wash up. It was liberating to stand naked and refreshed under a shade tree.

. . .

One afternoon on the new property, I decided to quit for the day. It was about 4:00 p.m., and the westerly sun was casting its rays of light along the eastern tree line. I had made good progress, and it felt good. As always, it was so quiet and peaceful. I felt I wanted to pray, to talk to God. I had a grass rake in my left hand and laid it on the ground. I knelt down onto my right knee, crossed both arms over my left thigh, and bowed my head. My words came easily today. I thanked Him for this beautiful property and a new start in life. It was at that moment, just after saying "Amen," that a loud explosive crack came from the east side of the tree line. I knew this sound well; it's a sound that gets your attention. A tree, that I had cut, had partially fallen and become hung up in a tall hickory, bending the tree like a bow and arrow. When this dense hickory snapped, the sound was sharp and clear. I couldn't help but think it was God saying you're welcome. But was this just a coincidence? I had had a few, what I would call, "spiritual experiences" in my life, and would like to believe they were orchestrated by God. But I struggled with these thoughts and feelings, I wanted to know or, at least, better understand them so not to be so doubtful.

· · ·

I was able to get the entire area cleared, firewood stacked, and brush burned. Our next step was to have the tree stumps removed. Mr. Robinson arrived early and immediately went to work. Mr. Robinson was in his seventies and loved being perched on top of his large Caterpillar bulldozer. I asked him at dinnertime how he learned to operate a bulldozer. He told me he was an infantry soldier during World War II on an island in the South Pacific battling the Japanese. A large military bulldozer was operating in front of them when its driver was shot by a sniper. With the sniper located and dealt with, an officer asked if anyone in the company knew how to operate a bulldozer. Mr. Robinson volunteered, he had grown up on a Tennessee farm and had experience with tractors. He felt he could learn, and he did. He operated it until the war was over. When he returned home, he decided to buy a used bulldozer and start a business.

Some of the stumps were easy to remove, as he only had to push the blade up against each stump and push it over and out of the ground. But some of the stumps were quite large. Mr. Robinson would pitch one side of the blade downward and lower it to the ground. He then would dig out next to the stump to cut enough roots and remove enough soil to loosen it. He would then push them out and back to the rear of our property and over a slight embankment. There was enough area to pile them up and not look unsightly. They would decompose, but this would take years, and we were fine with that.

Mr. Robinson was able to finish his work in about a week, working from daybreak to around 3:00 p.m., then it was home to tend to the farm. Many of the workers who helped with our build had a farm they tended to in the early mornings and evenings. Some grew vegetables or raised cattle or both.

Mr. Robinson did have his dinner routine: after a few slices of Oscar Mayer bologna and saltine crackers, he would lie on the seat of his pickup truck and take a 30-minute nap. We had interesting conversations about his life and the Baptist church he was very involved with. I always respected his nap time,. Eventually, yes, he invited me to visit his church.

· · ·

The next step on the property was to position the direction we wanted our house to face. I needed to go to town, about 8 miles, and buy some 2x4s to make batter boards. While I was loading the 2x4s, a man, a little older than me, who worked full-time in the lumber yard as a loader, walked over to assist me. He was very pleasant. Once again, he welcomed me to the community and asked if I had a church. He was the pastor of a small Baptist church just outside of town. This was my first experience encountering a part-time preacher or pastor. In Orlando, the few churches I became involved with had full-time pastors; I had never heard of a part-time preacher. He, like Mr. Robinson, invited me to his church. "You know, we do what's important to us." He meant that if it's important to me to attend church then I will. There was some wisdom in that statement, though it could also be applied to life in general.

· · ·

I'd only been in the community for about three months, but I noticed how friendly people were. I also noticed when at a stoplight, if I didn't head out immediately upon the light turning green, the person behind me didn't honk their horn. They simply waited until I moved forward. In Orlando, that usually wasn't the case. In my new town, there also seemed to be a church building on every corner, all heavily attended Sunday mornings and evenings, and Wednesday nights. I do remember that in Orlando, north on Magnolia Avenue from our firehouse, three churches stood side by side and another two just up the block. If responding during Sunday morning services, we would hold our sirens and air horns until we were past the church so as not to disturb their worship service.

. . .

I hired a small company that built custom houses to help with the building of our new home. I would pay them $12.50 per hour per crew member. I supplied the materials and donuts. They agreed to let me work alongside them as a crew member. Our house plans were drawn up in Orlando under the Southeast Building Code, which were quite specific and leaned on the heavier side of construction. Our county didn't have building codes. You could build a structure using flimsy lightweight material if you wanted too. The only inspections were for the rough in electrical wiring and septic tank and its drain field.

The lead carpenter was Jim. He had gone to school to obtain a contractor's license, and I was fortunate to have him leading our small team. Under his supervision, we built a plumb, level, sturdy structure using good materials. We were quite pleased how it turned out. After it was dried in, roof on, windows and doors hung, I would finish it myself. Spring was coming and the weather was beautiful for working outdoors; if the weather was bad, I worked indoors. It took a little over a year to finish the house, but our work produced a warm comfortable inviting home to live in.

. . .

I enjoyed finishing our home. I liked working with lumber, joining it together to produce a structural component or a decorative trim. I asked

Jim, Doug, and Ron, the three owners of the company if they needed any part-time help. They said they could use me, and I started working three days a week. I thoroughly enjoyed working on custom homes. At that time they didn't build speculative homes. So I got to meet and develop a relationship with the owners of their property and the dream home they envisioned. We built homes on sprawling acreage that was simply beautiful. Whether spring, summer, or fall, all made for nice weather to be outside. Especially in the fall and spring, the changing foliage was often spectacular. The downside was the winters. The temperatures could fall into the teens, requiring heavier clothing and gloves. But, even I, a Florida boy, bought appropriate rugged winter clothing and hung in there, working hard, staying warm.

I was fortunate to learn and understand how structures came together, how they were basically built. Back with the fire department, I had paid attention to instructors who taught building construction. I always felt this was important. Firefighters should know how structures were put together so if there was a fire and it was weakened in any way, we would have the knowledge to hopefully extricate ourselves before the building comes down around us. Jim helped me with reading the house plans and would sometimes say, "You're up," or "You're up to bat." He loved baseball, and this meant I would be cutting rafters that day or maybe laying out walls. Of course, he would always double check my measurements, and I was fine with that. I wanted to learn as much about construction as I wanted to learn about firefighting when I was a firefighter. I didn't want to make a mistake and cause us and the homeowner time or money.

One beautiful building site we worked on was on 165 acres. The large pasture where the house was going to sit was very fertile. The house sat about one quarter of a mile off the roadway and the traffic noise was buffered by a dense stand of white pine trees. The days when I would work, I'd arrive early and opened the gate at the road and drive to the construction site. My first duties were to turn on the electrical power at the temporary power pole, sending 240 volts of electricity along a heavy extension cord to another panel at the house where it was reduced to 120 volts. If it was cold, I'd start a campfire at our dinner and break area. A fire was always a welcome sight when arriving at daybreak; to warm up with a cup of coffee was a good start to the day. This house would be built like all the rest, stick-framed or platform-framed construction. This type of construction in our area was usually built on a crawl space or basement, and, usually, out of dimensional lumber. We built the roof systems using rafters, but rarely used wood trusses.

It was late in the fall when we worked on this particular house. If we were setting rafters, I always volunteered to work at the ridge. I didn't mind the height, was able to handle, with help, 16-foot rafters, and the view was spectacular. I would sometimes see deer just outside the tree line in the pasture. One late afternoon, a large buck stood by himself with imposing dignity. The house sat out in the open and had a 360-degree view that looked out over hills that were heavily forested with hardwoods, making for an expanse of beautiful reds, yellows, oranges, and greens. One other nice thing I remembered about being involved with the building of this house was that during the framing and drying in, it never rained. So, it never got wet; all framing and materials stayed dry, which rarely happens in our area.

One day after lunch, Doug suggested we look for arrowheads. The owner had turned a large section of pasture to let it sit for winter. I'd never had the opportunity to look for arrowheads before, so I joined the party. We started walking out into the freshly turned soil, and sure enough found an arrowhead, then another, and another. The first one I found was lying next to a clod of turned earth. I was taken back in time. According to Doug, this whole area would have been good hunting grounds for the Cherokee but possibly for folks way before them. We ended up with quite a few arrowheads that weren't chipped or broken.

I enjoyed working for this young couple. I helped design a well-organized laundry room and pantry. I had learned by taking the time to think things through and plan ahead, and this good habit made for a nice area that flowed well. I worked with one homeowner to build a laundry folding table next to the dryer. It became so useful for not only folding clothes but served as a workstation at times.

I also liked working with the homeowner. I wanted to build for them what they envisioned. If it was possible and structurally sound and if it was in their budget, why not? I liked working alongside them designing and drawing, coming up with working measurements that fit the space well. I was as satisfied doing this as I was accomplishing a goal with the fire department. I was now helping others but in a different way.

. . .

This small company was growing, and so I had an opportunity to work with different crew members, some young, some old. Depending on who I worked under or with could determine the quality of work and general ethical morality. Working under Doug, Jim, or Ron was never an issue, but the company had hired a few gentlemen that were difficult for me to work with. My first encounter with moral disappointment happened not too long after I started working for the company. I was helping with a large addition to a beautiful grand old house. I know it was in the summer because I remember Ron commenting on the noise made by the cicadas in the yard. Apparently, these were the seven-year cicadas, named after their predictably timed arrival. We broke for the dinner meal at 11:30 and found a place to sit in the large empty living room. There were quite a few tradespeople working this day, including plumbers, electricians, and carpenters, which made for a full room and possibly interesting conversations. As we settled in, one of the new lead carpenters said, "I have a joke for you." I didn't know him well; this was the first time working on the same job site. I had been told he was a pastor of a church in another county southwest of our small community. As I sat on a sheetrock bucket opening a can of tuna fish and small can of spinach with my P-38 can opener, the pastor began to tell his joke. He asked, "How many blacks does it take to build a road to heaven?" While I can remember that moment exactly, the sense of being caught off guard and taken back, to this day I don't remember the joke itself, the "punchline," the insult to African Americans. It seemed everyone laughed but me; I kept my head down, fiddling with my can opener, feeling embarrassed and uncomfortable. Very few black folks lived in this area; it was mostly white folks who rarely had an opportunity, or created an opportunity for themselves, to interact with them. I just never expected this type of joke to come from anyone there, much less a pastor. I viewed everyone in the room, except for me, as being righteous, or maybe virtuous is a better word, because of how religious they acted.

The entire afternoon I thought about what was said. When I got home that evening, I shared what happened with my wife. She wondered out loud if the pastor would use his joke on Sunday. Apparently, pastors often start their sermons with a joke. I wasn't aware of this, but my wife was; this was apparently quite common in this part of the country. She had attended a conservative Bible college and not only had a great wealth of knowledge about the Bible but also the different churches in this area. Once again, I was the ignorant one, striving to understand and learn. In the back of my mind, I was excited about moving to this region of the country. I had understood it to be very religious, but hopefully more godly than religious—folks who put others first and strived to follow the teachings of Jesus. But I didn't witness this at the dinner meal.

Not soon after this incident, I decided to attend what was, although I didn't know it at the time, a very conservative church denomination. After asking my wife's thoughts, I decided the Sunday evening service would be best for me. It was casual dress; I didn't own a dress suit that I felt was appropriate for church service. We settled into the middle of a pew and the service began. I expected the traditional worship songs, then someone to read a few excerpts from scripture, and a sermon preached towards the end. The sermon was on the book of Malachi, the last book in the Old Testament. Even though I knew where it was, I had to fumble through my Bible trying to find the correct passage, when those sitting next to me had already found it. I didn't know the Bible as well as my wife did, but I eventually was ready to read and hopefully understand it better.

The pastor stood in front of a thin wooden pulpit and delivered his message. He was well spoken and presented a good message. As we left the church, I stood in line to shake the pastor's hand and say thank you. With my wife standing next to me, I thanked him and then I said something that most likely didn't sit well with this pastor. I asked him if he'd listened to or heard of a certain well-known pastor. I could see his face change, and I knew I'd said something inappropriate. After we got to the car my wife explained my mistake. I was embarrassed but my thanks and praise for his sermon was genuine and heartfelt. What had to be explained was this pastor would never listen to the pastor I had mentioned. They were both quite conservative denominations, but their interpretation of the Bible was very different. I would soon learn that interpretation of scriptures was a big issue with the many different churches in the area.

. . .

In my new career as a carpenter, I was gaining experience and learning skills. One day, Ron explained and then demonstrated the correct steps to hang a door. His knowledge was invaluable, and to this day, I encounter few doors that are hung correctly. Ron was a Mennonite and had never shaved his beard, though he did keep it nicely trimmed.

One windy winter day, we were perched on the side of a southern-facing hip roof; wind was sweeping up the roof causing his beard to envelop his entire face. I smiled as Ron unsuccessfully tried to tuck it into the bib of this carpenter bib overalls. I truly loved working with Ron. He was intelligent and mindful. His slight pause before answering a question projected a thoughtful demeanor. One other quality Ron had acquired through the many years building houses was the ability to envision how something should look or turn out. Building custom homes was often challenging because they verged on complicated geometry. Ron had the ability to see and understand this in his mind.

I was helping him build a complicated soffit, at least in my mind. I was on an aluminum walk board installing the framing material, and Ron was a few feet away cutting the different parts. He had to walk me through it, asking for certain measurements and angles. As it got closer to a finished soffit, I started to understand how it was coming together. I had yet to learn that level of carpentry skills, but with Ron, Jim, and Doug's knowledge, I was acquiring and understanding more about this profession.

There was a lot to learn, especially to build a solid, tight, secure building. We strived in every way to produce neat tight connections. Window and door opening were framed level and plumb using straight material. The fasteners, such as nails and screws, were securely fastened in the correct location for a rigid solid support opening. To assemble a solid tightly connected rough opening, using headers, king studs, trimmers, cripples, and sill plates, was most rewarding. I knew my work would be covered over with some type of material, maybe sheetrock and paint, but I was proud of the work I accomplished and strived for perfection.

Working as a crew member with this small company had its advantages. I met different tradespeople to work around and ask questions about their profession. Most were small companies like ours, so I usually encountered the same folks. One small electrical company was run by a licensed electrician, the father, along with his sons and a daughter as his crew. They were quite good; they were knowledgeable, neat, and organized. I believe I was the only one who really noticed the hard work, skill, and knowledge of the daughter. She could handle the tools as well, if not better, than her brothers, and her knowledge of electricity was equal to her father's. But, I believe, because she was a woman, she wasn't respected. Other tradesmen would bypass her if they had electrical questions. It didn't appear to bother her; she may have had more insight into the mentality of males in this area.

. . .

One cool sunny morning in September we were framing a house on the fourteenth hole of a golf course. This course was laid out in a beautiful valley surrounded on three sides by rolling hills. Standing on scaffolding at the ridge, I knew in a little over a month the fall foliage would be at its peak. I was looking forward to being here and experiencing its beauty.

It was around 8:00 a.m. when Jeff, the outsides sales representative for the local contractor yard builder's center arrived. He told us he had heard on his car radio that an airplane had crashed into one of the World Trade Center towers. I immediately thought of the FDNY, and wondered how bad it was. Shortly after Jeff's report, he told us another plane had crashed into the other tower. We turned on our work sight radio to gain more information. We listened for about forty-five minutes but needed to get back to work. We checked for additional information throughout the day. That afternoon after work I went to the gym for a workout but found myself in front of the gym's television watching the towers collapse. I knew I would know some of the firefighters who had died. When the names of the firefighters who died started to become public, my sadness intensified. I had met some of them, talked with them, and had asked them questions when I visited their departments in the 1970s and '80s. Some were the sons of firefighters who had recently retired as I had.

One firefighter I had the honor to meet and spend countless hours talking with was John Vigiano. I had met him when he was the lieutenant of Rescue Company 2 in Brooklyn. He lost two sons on September 11: John Jr., a FDNY firefighter, and Joe, an NYPD detective.

Another firefighter, Lee Ielpi, also a member of Rescue Company 2, lost his son Jonathan of Squad 288 when the towers collapsed.

December 11, 2001, was a cool gray workday. Just before quitting time, Ron and I were at the peak of a roof wanting to finish drying it in. We had a few more 1x12 pine sheeting boards to install as well as number 30 felt paper to button-cap down to keep the rain and snow from entering. We could feel the rain getting close; the flat black color of the clouds extended out in every direction. They were dense and gave the appearance they may have been quite thick. These clouds seemed extremely low, and sitting at the ridge, we felt we could almost reach up and touch them.

Ron looked at the clouds and said, "That cloud looks like a fire hat." He meant it look like a fire helmet. As he pointed up and westward, I too could see a perfectly proportioned shape of a leather New Yorker–style fire helmet. With the flat black color of the clouds, it looked like it had been in a fire with heavy carbon buildup. I immediately thought of Jonathan, and his father who searched daily, hoping to find and recover his remains. Turning my head northward, I saw in the far distance a small hole in the clouds, and watched a tight crisp ray of bright sunshine make its way to the ground. In that beam of sunshine, I saw and felt in my soul a hope, a peacefulness, that Jonathan was now at peace. Ron had also experienced what I saw, though it only lasted a short while, a few seconds at most.

Ron and my thoughts were interrupted when our last board was pushed between the rafters and ridge. We quickly nailed it down and ran a 36-inch-wide roll of felt paper the length of the entire ridge. As large heavy raindrops started pelting the felt paper, we carefully climbed down. By now the entire crew had left and only Ron and I remained. We said goodbye and headed to our trucks.

Just as I got settled in, started the truck, heater on, I sat there for a few minutes. I couldn't help but think about what had just happened. It was now raining steady, and I would be careful driving the forty-five minutes to my home. I would have time to reflect on what had happened that evening along with other unusual experiences I'd encountered. I remember it raining throughout the night, but I don't remember the next day. A few days later, I read that Jonathan's remains had been found late in the evening on December 11, 2001.

. . .

In building my new woodworking shop, I had a separate monolithic concrete slab poured when our garage floor was poured. I took the time to run adequate electrical service and water to it. One nice Saturday, I had Jim, Ron, and Ron's two sons help frame and raise 10-foot exterior walls. This went rather quickly, and we were done by lunch. We had a wonderful dinner on a picnic table in the backyard. To eat a comfort meal with kind friends on a beautiful day was nice.

Since I wanted an unobstructed open work area, I ordered wood trusses for the roof. Once again on a pleasant Saturday morning I had Jim, Ron and his sons out to help with the installation of the trusses. We made quick work of the trusses and we're able to sheet the entire roof with plywood and secure with felt paper. It was now dried in; I would now finish it myself.

. . .

I continued to work three days a week for the construction company and also worked three days on my woodshop. I enjoyed the work and was learning a great deal. Another talented carpenter I enjoyed working with was Jim Jernigan, who also happened to be a Vietnam veteran. He was an army engineer who built military instillations throughout South Vietnam. He was methodical and knew his trade well. I knew I could also learn a great deal from him, but he was mostly involved in the finish carpenter end of the home build. Where I was being used for the framing portion, Jim was used for intricate details of fine cabinetry, crown molding, decorative trim, etc. For years I was only involved with the framing portion, but as time went by, I got the opportunity to assist Jim. I looked at it as being his apprentice. Whether natural finished hardwoods or painted poplar wood his connections were precisely joined together making for a beautiful piece of work. I was impressed as well as the homeowners. Jim produced beautiful, finished cabinets, built in hutches, etc. I knew to get to his level would take time, experience, and knowledge, something I was willing to invest in. Jim took side jobs on the weekends and sometimes hired me to assist him. I usually jumped at the chance, and we became good friends. He and his wife Sandi raised a large garden, and they would give us green beans, okra, potatoes, corn, or whatever they were growing throughout the year.

Like with the military and fire department, I watched and listened, slowly learning and gaining those skills that produced a higher level of carpenter. A hammer, skill saw, tape measure was as comfortable in my hands as the M60 machine gun or the Partner K1200 power saw.

As I gained experience and knowledge, I was also experiencing carpenter work that wasn't done to the quality I felt should be the norm for this area. It seemed to me that most of the men I worked with would never use profanity. They often talked religiously, sung spiritual songs, and sometimes quoted scripture. They would never miss a church service, even if they were out of town. But their quality of workmanship didn't project those same moral ethics. I hadn't experienced this behavior before, and I wasn't sure how to act and work around it. If these men and some women I've met were a representation of "Christianity," I was having difficulty understanding this behavior.

There was no doubt they believed that Jesus was the son of God, and this Jesus came upon this earth to save humanity. But it appeared to me that that was all they felt Jesus was for. I felt Jesus was more than just a savior; he walked this earth and taught and showed humanity how he wanted us to live together. It's written clearly in the fifth, sixth, and seventh chapters of the book of Matthew. Maybe some felt it wasn't important to read, and if they did, they may have a different interpretation of those chapters.

I wasn't having thoughts that we'd made a mistake moving to this area. I knew in my heart I would rather live in Tennessee than in Orlando. But I was feeling a sentimental goodness for Orlando, maybe because I'd lived there longer. When I reflect on my time in Orlando, I see a goodness in that community, a goodness that could surpass our new community.

. . .

As my carpenter skills progressed, I was given assignments to finish a few unfinished items in the homes we built. My first was to install oak shoe molding throughout the house. This was a fairly straightforward job, but there were some techniques I had learned from Ron and Jim to ensure that I'd install it properly.

The home wasn't fully furnished, but the homeowners had moved in. They were a pleasant couple a little younger than me. Their home was two stories with red-oak hardwood flooring; there was no carpeting at all. I had a fair amount of work to complete but was fine working by myself and looked at is as my first job on my own. Instead of brick, commonly used here, it was circular size stone randomly stacked with masonry joints. With steep pitched rooflines it looked like an English stone cottage set in the woods. All interior trim was painted white. The baseboards were 6 inches high, and all doorways and case opening had plinth blocks. The homeowner asked if I would return the shoe molding back to itself, meaning not to cut a short angle, maybe a half inch, at the end of the shoe molding when it dies into the plinth block. I never cared for this look; returning it looks more finished, but some homeowners prefer the angle cut. The angle cut is faster, but you still have to stain or paint the section cut off. As with the return, if you make a nice connection, it doesn't need any attention except to fill a nail hole. I'd usually glue the small return piece to the end of the shoe molding, avoiding a nail. But if I had to use a nail, I used a pneumatic pin nailer at its end, no filling required.

I also used a coping saw to cut the profile of the shoe molding where it meets at an inside corner. The coping cut always fits together nicely, as opposed to cutting two angles in each end piece. If the degree angle of the corner isn't an exact 90 degrees, it will leave an opening that doesn't look neat and professional. I've heard some carpenters say, "You'll never see it," or "It's in a corner with furniture up against it." But I felt it was important to me and the homeowner to do the best job possible. If having to splice two pieces of molding together, such as for a long wall, I tried my best to make the connections as inconspicuous as possible.

The shoe molding was stained and finished to match the flooring. It was neatly arranged by length in the garage. This was very helpful for measuring, because the goal is to install it with the least number of seams. I sawed in the garage and made many trips inside for installation, but it came out beautifully and the homeowner and I were pleased with the nice, neat job.

Working on this home I got to eat lunch and take breaks with the homeowners. I found this interesting and fun. You can learn a lot by listening to people's lives and their involvement in this small community.

I also had the opportunity to meet a few interior decorators when they arrived on the job site. Ellie was cool and had a wonderful eye for color and details. She once had the painters paint a dining room a dark chocolate brown. I was skeptical but that's what she and the homeowner decided. I had the opportunity to come back to this home to finish a few projects. After seeing the finished dining room with furniture, lighting, and curtains, I was truly amazed. It was warm, beautiful, and inviting. Ellie hit a home run in that room.

Ellie and her family moved to this area around the same time we had. Her interior design company was doing well and was quite respected. With her eye for space and detail, I knew I could learn much from her. I was producing nice, neat work, but it was from plans. I didn't have the artist's eye like Ellie had. I asked her if she had any side work that I may be able to help her with. She said she did, and I started to learn that side of the profession.

I eventually made the decision to venture out on my own. I had acquired a fair number of tools of the trade and had a reliable clean work truck. When applying for the business license the lady asked what the name of my business was. I had been thinking about this. I had previously worked for a woman who had difficulty getting the builder back to finish a few items that should have been finished with her home build. She was having an open house for her neighbors and wanted everything complete. When I had finished all items on her "punch list," she said to me, "You came to my rescue." I had come to her rescue in a way, and since I was involved with rescue on the fire department and in Vietnam, I wondered about naming my company to accompany this theme. One of the most rewarding accomplishments when I was in Vietnam was to evacuate wounded from the battlefield. Often our helicopters were closer than a DUSTOFF medical helicopter; we never hesitated to do our best to rescue the wounded. I felt, and I'm quite certain other aviators would agree, we would risk life and helicopter to save the life of an American combat soldier; they were that respected. I decided to name my company DUSTOFF Construction Company. I felt if you were a military veteran, you would know the meaning of DUSTOFF, and if not, I would hope the name would represent cleanliness or imply that I'd take the time to dust off or vacuum my work. Whatever way it was taken I was proud to have selected that name.

My tools were quality. I owe that to my mother. She always encouraged me, if possible, to buy quality products that would hold up and give years of service. Since most of my work would be inside of structures or homes, I used my older stepladders for outside work and bought a nice complement of sturdy ladders to be used only on inside jobs. They were also very stable to support long clean aluminum walk boards. I had seen tradesman bring stepladders into a nice clean home with dried mud caked on its feet, waiting to be bumped and fall off. I felt this was unprofessional. I now had two tool work belts, one was setup for framing, the other for finish carpentry. It wasn't as bulky as the framing belt so as not to get caught on furniture. I also bought some khaki pleated trousers and different colored collared tee shirts with DUSTOFF Construction Company embroidered in small letters on the left chest. I wore a soft sole work shoe instead of a big clunky boot with an aggressive sole that would trap mud and dirt. I felt this was the image I wanted in a finished carpenter. I would keep my truck clean and polished. Your truck and tools say a lot about the tradesperson.

I truly liked working by myself. I found I could best concentrate without loud music and pointless talk distracting me. I charged a modest hourly rate. The homeowner paid for the materials. I never had anyone question my hours, and I built a reputation of integrity that I was proud of.

I enjoyed the challenges involved in this work. It wasn't at all about the money but the satisfaction of accomplishment. More and more of my work involved unusual builds. I found this could be somewhat stressful but also very challenging to figure out how to accomplish. As I now reflect, I get as much satisfaction out of figuring out how to accomplish a task as I do with the finish product. I was now in my third profession—military, fire department, and now carpentry. They were all equally challenging and rewarding in different ways.

. . .

One memorable job during my last years in my carpenter career lasted about three years. I was hired by a beautiful family to finish a three-story town house just off the town square. They were living at their lake house at the time, and since their children were now close to middle and high school, they wanted to move to town. They bought an old brick telephone company building and had its exterior completely restored with new brick, French casement windows, and stone parapets. I started on the top floor, which would be their residence, and worked my way down. Fortunately, they installed an elevator that greatly helped with moving tools and materials. The focus of the home was a French theme. They loved French art and French-style architecture, quite challenging for me.

The homeowners were very accommodating and thoughtful. They provided heat in the winter and air conditioning in the summer with a constant relative humidity around 35 to 40 percent. This was quite valuable and necessary because of the dimensions of material used and the close tolerances required. It really was a finished carpenter's dream. The building was secure; I had a key and could leave my tools set up. As I reflect on this project now, I feel proud I was able to give the homeowner exactly what they had envisioned. I knew what had to be accomplished behind the scenes to get to the beautiful, detailed finish. I was fortunate to have the opportunity to work alongside talented stone masons, metal workers, and blacksmiths. Also, a father-and-son team who installed decorative plaster to the ceilings were quite interesting to get to know. They had immigrated from Russia and now lived in Nashville. Their work was truly amazing.

. . .

Next door to the town house was a church. The two buildings were only about 10 to 12 feet apart. In time, I would meet the pastor, assistant pastor, and a few members of the congregation. They were friendly and invited me to Sunday services. I had heard how beautiful the sanctuary was and one afternoon after work I walked out the back door of the town house walked a few paces and entered through the side door of the church. Entering the sanctuary, I was moved by its beauty and warmth. This day the westerly sun was shining through the stained-glass windows casting beautiful colors on the butternut wood pews. The entire space was inviting, peaceful, and solemn. Some of the radiators were giving off a faint clicking sound as they produced heat. I walked to the front pew, sat, and talked to God. This became somewhat of a routine I looked forward too.

One Monday morning, a week before Easter Sunday, I was entering the town house for work when I saw Denna, the servant minister for the church. She asked if I was going to attend Holy Week services. I wasn't familiar with this and expressed my interest. She told me at this time of year the Presbyterian Church across the street offered what had become known as Holy Week. This church would invite five pastors from different local churches to preach a short sermon on Jesus's last week, terminating on Good Friday. The service starts at noon and lasted thirty minutes, and then lunch was served. She invited me to attend, and I did. Just before noon I walked out the front door of the town house, crossed the street, and entered the sanctuary of the church. The condensed service was well orchestrated, and every pew was full. From Monday to Good Friday, I heard five different pastors give well-thought-out sermons. Denna's pastor preached on Thursday, and she'd especially wanted me to meet and hear him. I liked his message and sincere calm demeanor, and I decided to attend his Sunday morning service.

At that point in my life, I didn't own a suit or even a nice dress jacket to wear to church. I was brought up to always dress up for church. God was inviting us into his earthly home, and as invited guests we should respond with appreciation and look our best. Maybe that was the Catholic way, or the way I understood it, but I did love God enough to at least dress for him. I went to Belk, a department store in town, and bought a coat, slacks, shirt, tie, belt, and shoes.

My first Sunday service was an eye-opener. I arrived early, and after picking up a church bulletin, I selected a pew about halfway back from the altar. I was always taught by my father that since pews were often placed close together, it's best to enter the pew and proceed to the middle. That way, others don't have to climb over you. This made sense, but I encountered folks who wanted to sit at the end, so they either had to get up and exit the pew or you had to maneuver past them. As time got closer for the service, folks began to fill the sanctuary. I wasn't prepared for the noise. Once again, I was taught church was a solemn holy space, so when entering a church sanctuary, you were to be quiet and respectful. It was a place for prayer and worship, to meditate on the Lord. Conversation was to be held in the foyer or lobby. I brought my Bible, small notebook, and pencil.

Arriving early also gave me time to find the scripture reading and to find the songs to be song in the hymnal. Once settled in, I looked over the scripture reading. There were usually two—one from the Old Testament and one from the New. I then placed a bookmark in my Bible to find them. A few folks came to welcome me but not as many as I expected (and somewhat dreaded). I had always felt peace and warmth in an empty sanctuary, but once it was filled with people that sometimes changed. I was feeling somewhat out of place, wondering if attending church was right for me.

Though, overall, I did enjoy the service; I liked the contemporary Christian music, and the sermon was relevant. After the benediction I sat to reflect, pray, and jot down any notes in my notebook. I also wanted to let those around me exit first before I did. I felt this may be a church suited for me. Not too far right or left, pretty much in the middle, a nice balance.

Since they offered two services, I decided to attend the first, thinking it would be less attended, I was incorrect. As I was leaving, I was invited by a few folks to attend their Bible study class. I didn't know it at the time, but there were many different classes that were offered, with different points of view in regard to social issues. I knew I would not attend a class; I was still fearful I would be asked to read out loud and embarrass myself. I thanked them and walked up the street to a pastry shop for a blueberry muffin and coffee. I enjoyed sitting at a window seat enjoying the freshly baked muffin and reviewing my notes. I did write one interesting observation; I didn't see anyone bring a Bible. When time for the scripture reading some reached forward to remove the new crisp Bible in front of them but most only listened to the reading by the lector or reader. I may have brought attention to myself with my Bible in my hand, I didn't want that. But I did feel the Bible was important to the service and decided I would continue to bring it, along with my notebook.

. . .

The town house project was slowly making headway. With so many talented craftspeople working side by side to produce a beautiful space it took not only each of their talents but also timing was important to keep everything flowing. Since I was the only carpenter, I was consulted with on most every move. I didn't mind the added responsibility; I knew it was important if this project was to be a success. I enjoyed working with all the different trades and felt we were a close team, all striving for a common goal. Once again, I was seeing a group of people working together to accomplish a goal. Though in the army, or on the fire department we strived to accomplish a goal that ultimately saved lives or property, but here it was to produce a grandeur of beauty and fine craftsmanship. I loved being on a team where everyone was excited to give their all for the good of the project and for the team. I never saw any arrogance; these folks just didn't have that trait within them.

I had now been working in the trade for almost fifteen years. My knees had started to give me problems and I would guess because of the years spent on them. I had finished my part on two of the three floors of the town house, and this was a good stopping point to take a break and have knee replacement. My thought was to have one replaced and after recovery have the other. I didn't feel rushed to have both done at the same time and glad I didn't. For reasons I'll most likely never know, the first knee replacement didn't go well; it became infected. It took close to a year to resolve this problem, but thankfully it didn't turn out even worse.

I had initially planned during my recovery time to read and study the Bible, which I did when I wasn't sick fighting the infection. I bought a set of Bible commentaries written by William Barclay, and along with the help of the internet, I dove in. One of the first things I encountered was the meaning of light and the sounds of trumpets. Light was often referred to as God, and sounds of trumpets referred to sounding an alert, sending a message. Thinking back to October 1972, that is what I had experienced. I wondered if the extremely bright white light was God's presence, and the sound of a horn or trumpet was God telling me that he'd heard my request. This study began in October 2012, forty years after I had laid on my bunk at the firehouse. In my study, I came to understand "forty" was laced throughout the Bible. But what hit me the hardest was that the Israelites wondered forty years in a wilderness after their disobedience. I understood that I had also been disobedient. I knew I was knowingly and unknowingly sinning in my forty-year block of time, and that I deserved the same discipline. Now reflecting on those forty years, I experienced a little joy, but mostly heartache and pain. Yet more important it was a teaching series, a time to learn about the person I was still growing into.

About two years after my first knee replacement, I had the other knee replaced, a successful surgery this time. Having had three operations on my first knee, however, I was left with limited range of motion that would later hinder me on jobsites. I would often trip as I was not able to fully lift my leg to step over something. Because I was often on ladders and using walk boards, I needed two stable legs to support myself. Tripping or stumbling at floor level was one thing. Standing on a ladder or perched high on scaffolding was something else. I decided it was time to retire from jobsites. I could still build projects in my workshop, and, thankfully, I still enjoyed that immensely.

. . .

I was at the point that I wanted to become more involved in the church. As far back as basic training, I felt "church" was important but for reasons I don't fully understand, but didn't or couldn't attend.

The pastor of the church, who also loved woodworking, asked if I would build a few items for the church. And the choir director asked if I could build some stage props. I also did some church renovation. I was glad to be able to help.

I also decided to volunteer at the food pantry. It was open from 2:30 p.m. to 6:00 p.m. on Tuesdays. I met with Kathy, the coordinator of what she referred to as "the boots on the ground" section. She assigned me to be a runner. Kathy had utmost compassion for the recipients. She often showed it with a hug, prayer, or heartfelt conversation. I also loved her concern and passion for the ministry, and felt a love for her heart. I too wanted a heart like her's.

My job as a runner was to fill food orders and deliver them to the recipients. If they were disabled, or of poor health I would carry them to their means of transportation. Some had to walk, some rode the bus, some came as a group in one car, and some had their own vehicles.

The way our pantry worked at that time, a recipient had to first sign up to be eligible to receive items. They had to live within the same county as the church and produce two valid address verifications, such as a rent receipt and an electricity or water bill. Once they met these requirements, they were given a small pantry card that included the total number of adults and children in their families.

Usually around 1:00 p.m., a line would start to form at the front door of the sanctuary. When the pantry opened, they would present their card to one of the three female staff volunteers and their names would be checked off under today's date. This checklist was only used to determine the number of folks who came through weekly, so as to determine how much food or household items to have on hand.

These polite and respectful volunteers would hand each recipient a shopping list, with their name written on it. At the top right of the list was the number of members in their family that would determine the number of items to give them. Each week's shopping list had fifteen different items printed on it. The recipient could select ten of the fifteen. They would then exit the sanctuary and walk downstairs to the church basement where the pantry was located.

After entering through the pantry door, the recipient would place their shopping list in a basket, one on top of the other. This is where I would help with the process, I would reach down and secure the bottom list and start to fill the order on this list. All items would be placed in plastic bags, and I would then walk back out to the recipient waiting area and hand off the bags. It took months to recognize faces and acquire a trusting rapport with the recipients. I found my job most rewarding and usually always carried their items out to their transportation. This gave me time to get to know them better, to understand their current situation and how they arrived at that point in their lives. My eyes were opened, and I was understanding these folks that were often looked down upon. But it was exhausting, and I often went home tired and worn out. On my drive home I would often pray for the people I'd helped that day, and understood just how fortunate I was to have a nice warm home and nutritious food to eat.

I worked with a good team of mostly senior folks. Everyone had their assignment or duties, and all worked well together. It was often very busy and quite tiresome, but I was proud of the hard work everyone did. There were some volunteers with years of experience, who were truly lovely and compassionate people who understood our recipients and how the pantry was critical for them and their families. They were pillars and greatly respected.

One such woman was Per, she had been at the pantry for years and became a mentor to me. She was very kind and thoughtful, and treated all recipients equally with love, compassion, and respect.

One Tuesday we were unusually busy. Though rarely was there a slow day, most days around 4:30 there was a lull, then from 5:00 to 6:00 we'd get busy again. So that day when 4:30 rolled around, I took time to sit for a few minutes. I wasn't sitting long when an African American couple, looking to be in their seventies, walked through the door. I always enjoyed seeing them because they were always congenial and appreciative. They usually went over to Per, handed her their grocery list, and the three of them sat close together on an old, discarded church pew. As I looked on, I was moved by the compassion and focus Per had for them. I soon understood they were illiterate so each week Per would quietly read the food choices and with pencil in hand she filled out their list. They talked between themselves to select their ten items. As I watched quietly from my inconspicuous seat, I saw compassion, love, and dignity conveyed to them from Per. As they stood, she handed them their list, and they all hugged. It was a moving site, a blonde, blue-eyed white woman and African Americans embracing, a simple act of acceptance and respect. Fifty-five years before this would have been considered a breach of social behavior. That day Per not only fed those in need, but also ministered to their soul and mine as well.

As I continued to work at the pantry, I was asked to help Per and Charleen with signing up new recipients. Often, Charleen and Per were overwhelmed with the volume of folks needing to sign up. This is when I would step up to assist.

One afternoon a young girl walked through the door with a baby in her arms. I could tell she was unfamiliar and uncomfortable with the surroundings. I asked if I could help her. She asked if she could get baby food for her daughter. I told her that I would be happy to assist her. I had her sit down in a small wooden chair next to a small desk. Because some people felt embarrassed having to resort to a food pantry, Per, Charleen, and I always did our best to make all new recipients feel comfortable.

I asked her if she would fill out a small information card with her name, address, and how many were in her family. If they had children, could she please write down their ages.

I could see she was having trouble holding the small child and writing so I asked her if I could help her by filling out the card for her. She gave me her name, and I asked about the child. She told me her daughter was only a few months old. I also asked if there were any others in the family. Looking at her beautiful little girl, I asked about the father. She simply shook her heard. I then asked her, if he helps financially, and she said he didn't. I wrote "one adult" on the card and "one child." I then turned the card around so she could easily sign it.

I noticed she was left-handed and thought of my sister who is also left-handed. My sister is extremely smart, and, as I've mentioned, it seems like most left-handed people are. I told her we could provide baby food and sometimes disposable diapers. Since I had previously asked her if she lived in this county, she produced the two documents needed by the church to receive help. I noticed her documents provided her parents' address. This wasn't an issue, at least in my mind, but as we talked, I sensed her parents may not be willing to accept her situation.

I asked her age and if she was still in school. She told me she just turned sixteen and her parents made her quit school to get a job and provide for her baby. My heart sank; I had compassion and sorrow for her as I knew her life would become extremely difficult. I did my best to be encouraging and hopeful, but I had too many years of life experiences and felt her and her child's life would be an uphill struggle.

We filled out a grocery list, and I added a few extra items. She did have a ride this day, but she wasn't sure if she could get one next Tuesday. I walked her out and told the lady driving how thankful I was for her and hoped she could get help with transportation in the future.

This meeting was sad and yet there were so many sad situations we encountered. When I returned home that evening, I shared this meeting with my wife. As we talked, it hit me, if it wasn't for my insecurities and low self-esteem, my fifteen-year-old hormones could have easily got me into a similar situation.

Next Tuesday, I kept an eye out for the young girl, but she didn't return. This happened sometimes, and I wondered why.

· · ·

Attending church was going well, I enjoyed the sermons and songs. I did search for just the right place to sit, a place I felt comfortable. I tried sitting in different sections, front, middle, rear, and the balcony. I found the balcony was too disruptive, too much commotion, making it hard to hear and concentrate. Selecting the rear or middle of the church was a disruption to the folks who seemed to have assigned seats. I felt uncomfortable breaking up folks who liked to sit together.

I found that the front of the church, the second pew, was best for me. When I attended classes at the fire department, I tried to sit at the front desks or tables. These were usually always open, and I could see and hear well. Back then, photo slides were used to project images on a screen, and

I was able to see them well. I liked it, since I was excited to learn about firefighting. I now felt learning about God was equally important, maybe even more, so why not sit up front. I was able to tune out what was going on behind me and focus on the service. Usually, the first few pews were sparsely occupied so I didn't have to climb over anyone or felt like I was taking anyone's seat. Sitting close to the alter was also nice for enjoying the beautiful music directed by Kathy, the chorus director. Martha Sue was magnificent behind the organ, and both she and Kathy were brilliant on the piano.

· · ·

One weekday morning I was at church for the funeral for one of its members. Standing outside on the sidewalk that led to the front doors of the church I recognized many of the folks gathered for the service. All were dressed in their finest clothing. Then I noticed Linda, the church custodian, setting orange traffic cones in the street. She was a petite middle-aged woman, always polite, with a gentle quiet demeanor. She always wore slightly oversized T-shirts that draped down over her slacks. I had the opportunity to get to know her and knew she had seen and experienced much heartache in her life. Her unassuming demeanor made her somewhat invisible. Standing there were prominent leaders of the community, pastors, assistant pastors, and well-off folks, a lot of talking and some posturing. Yet there moves Linda. To some she may be considered least or less than, an $8.00-an-hour employee, diligently setting orange traffic cones. As I take in this scene, I can't help to think, out of all of those assembled there, Linda may just be the godliest. In my eyes, this woman standing in the rain-soaked street setting traffic cones was the epitome of Jesus.

· · ·

A member who I had met soon after I started going to services, asked if I would be interested in attending a new Sunday school class that he and his wife were starting. He explained their ideas and thoughts for the class, and it sounded like a good fit for me. I did know there were about eight different Sunday school classes offered, ranging from liberal to conservative. I had become comfortable and brave enough to attend these different classes to see what they taught. Most were hum drum, not wanting to explore the deeper side of theology. Some of these classes started out reading a passage with the plan to go deeper into the passage and meaning but soon the conversation turned secular and into everyday conversation.

One very popular class, the one with the highest attendance numbers at the time, was called the "backsliders." I felt quite certain it leaned on the conservative side. They would say the pledge of allegiance at the beginning of class and sing patriotic songs. Many military veterans were in this class. One Sunday during Veterans Day weekend, I came to church to be met in the narthex by picture after picture of church veterans in their dress uniform, metals displayed across their chest. I felt uncomfortable seeing this; I too was a veteran but to display a military picture of myself in this context seemed inappropriate in a church.

One member of this class shared with me that a well-educated lady, also from this class, was an authority on the Muslim religion and was going to speak next Sunday. I thought it would be interesting to learn more about this religion. The following Sunday I was extremely disappointed in her presentation. Her tone and accusations were meant to be demeaning, even combative, to the folks who were Muslim and to the religion of Islam. It wasn't at all educational. As I sat listening, I thought of Jesus and of the building I was in, but I felt like I was in a war room. I excused myself to my friend and left. I was very bothered by what I experienced and knew I saw another side of the Christian religious community that didn't sit right with me.

• • •

I attended a service a few weeks before Christmas. The entire service was orchestrated around the birth of Jesus. It was a grand production put together by the music department. I arrived early as usual but because this was a production involving the children of the church it was unusually full. The front four pews were reserved for the handbell musicians and for the children participating in the program. So I reversed direction and walked back to the first pew that had open seats. I entered but was told they were being saved. I said OK, went to the pew directly behind it, and asked a lady if the seats beside her were taken. She said they were but that I could sit at the end. I knew others in this area heard our exchange, and I was feeling embarrassed. These folks I interacted with were longtime members. I had been at the church for a while but not feeling welcomed. I sat down at the end of the pew; there was a comfortable space to seat two more people, maybe even three (but it would be tight). I felt uncomfortable sitting at the very end and not next to the lady. I also felt uncomfortable knowing the numerous people standing next to me in the aisle searching for seats. The husband of the lady arrived and sat next to her but there was still room for two other people between him and me. A young lady arrived with a small child and asked if the seats were taken between me and the man. I said they were, but not thinking, I should have asked the man if others were still coming for the seats next to him. I'm quite certain they heard our exchange, but neither the man nor the lady said a word. I stood up and offered my seat to her and her son, but she declined my offer and quickly escorted her son back through the crowd of people. I was now even more embarrassed and ashamed of how this was playing out.

The organ began to play signaling the beginning of the service. The once crowded aisle disappeared to the back of the church. I wish I would have been more forceful in communicating to the young woman and child to take my seat. I could possibly find another or just leave; I was that upset. I'm thinking the young woman may have had an older child in the production or maybe had been invited to visit the church for this children's production. Either way I did a poor job of making them feel welcome. As the music played, I gazed forward to the large cross on the wall in front of the sanctuary and thought of Jesus and how he must feel. I felt so much love and compassion for him, yet I let him down today. The seats next to me were unoccupied the entire service; to this day I've continue to feel sad for the young lady and small child.

· · ·

One Saturday morning I was working in my woodshop when a car pulled up, and two nicely dressed gentleman stepped out. Because it was

Saturday, and they were in their nice attire carrying bibles in their hands, I knew they were Jehovah's Witnesses. I greeted them, and they were sincerely friendly and smiling kindly. They introduced themselves and I to them. They asked if I had time to talk, and I said I did and invited them into the shop. I had some comfortable chairs and a few stools to offer them. I did try to keep the area where we sat free of sawdust; I apologized anyway for any dust, but they were fine with it. I sat them in the two comfortable chairs, and I took a stool. One of the gentlemen was in his eighties and the other was maybe in his fifties.

I had known a little about Jehovah's Witnesses due to my wife's study of the Bible and different religions. At this point, I'd had only a few conversations with her, but one fact stood out: they did not believe Jesus was God, only God's son. My reading, or interpretation, of the Bible, was that Jesus is God who came to this earth in the form of a human being to teach and show us how we should live with our fellow human beings. This had been my belief, but what I found with talking to the Jehovah's Witnesses was that their beliefs were not the same as mine. Their job, or assignment, was to educate me and convince me that I was incorrect. This was one of the problems I found with the Bible. There are many different interpretations. One other thought or question I had about the book was this: Is it the divine word of God, given to man to record, or was it written by man and God had no say so in it?

This first meeting lasted exactly an hour. They were considerate with my time, not to overwhelm me with their presentation. Before they left, they asked if they could return next Saturday. I said yes and told them I'd have coffee ready. After they left, I reflected on our conversation, and it came to me that our time together centered around interpretation. If we both believed there was a God, and strived to live a godly life, what did it matter?

The next Saturday they were punctual, and once again we sat in the workshop drinking coffee and talking. I was quite sure they felt they had a convert and were pleased. I don't believe I ever gave them that impression; I just wanted to understand their interpretation of the Bible.

I had previously been educated by my wife that the Jehovah's Witnesses published their own Bible. I was starting to notice that every question I asked these nice folks prompted them to flip through their well-worn Bible and pull a verse or verses from it, whether or not it answered my question. I was longing for heartfelt conversations about those controversial and hard-to-understand writings in the Bible.

After about six months of visits, I was sufficiently educated about the beliefs of their religion. I told them what pleasant and kind folks they were and that I respected their interpretation of their Bible. I admired their dedication to their church and study. Then I shared the one problem I had with their religion: accepting their interpretation that Jesus was not God. I confessed to them my interpretation, and that I wanted to believe God did walk this earth as a human being by the name of Jesus to show us the correct way to live. I just couldn't believe anything other than that. I also told them if I ever got the opportunity to speak with Jesus, he might say with a smile on my face, "Oh Bill, I want to thank you for believing I was God in the flesh and honoring me in that way, but the truth is I'm really only his son, but thanks again for your belief and love." If I'm wrong, does it matter? I don't think God would be jealous. Wouldn't he be proud of his son and what he sacrificed for all of humanity. After this last conversation the Jehovah's Witnesses didn't return for years. One Saturday morning they drove up again with their wives. We had a nice conversation but not about the Bible or religion.

. . .

The church I had been attending was starting to show an ugly side. I was seeing a prideful self-importance in some of the members. I also felt the church had more of a social club atmosphere than that of a spiritual meeting place. This didn't apply to everyone, but I felt it applied to far too many for a house of worship, a structure that was built to worship God, as well as a place that is supposed to encourage us to strive to have a heart similar to Jesus's.

I wasn't seeing the pastors preaching Jesus's values. Most sermons were plain vanilla, so to speak, so as not to disrupt, or ruffle the feathers of, the congregation. How can hearts and minds be changed without being instructed and nourished by the teachings of Jesus? I'm just not sure most folks care about learning more about his teachings. I read this from

William Barclay: "There are people who feel no need to look deeper into who Jesus is. Let them remain forever undisturbed in the sweet simplicity of their faith." I have been around many folks who feel this way. Is it terribly wrong? I can't be judgmental; I'm only expressing what I'm seeing. We as humans are all different in many ways, especially when it comes to what we believe.

With what I was seeing I decided to take some time off from the church and visit other churches in the area. I selected a different church each Sunday, and if I felt it may be a good fit, I would return. After close to a year, I hadn't found a Christian church I felt could teach and nourish me.

I knew I wasn't a deep thinker by definition: "a person whose thoughts are profound; and intellectual." Yet I often pondered spiritual matters and yearned for deeper understanding. I was still hoping to find a church brave enough to dive deeper into controversial issues.

With the COVID pandemic gaining momentum and so much misinformation about the virus, I felt it was best to stay home on Sundays. I could watch services throughout the world on YouTube. This became my worship service, and it still is to this day.

. . .

With the pandemic and our country's political divide I found myself pouring myself into prayer. I was earnestly praying more, not only to God but also for humanity worldwide. I so wanted folks to put aside their differences and come together for the common good of all. But I was seeing more division, more anger, hostility, and violence. I was neither politically far left or right; I considered myself mainly in the middle. Which way I leaned, depended on the issue. I liked this balance, and I was willing to listen to and do my best to understand both sides of an issue or misunderstanding. But what I was seeing was that the two sides were so entrenched in their beliefs, even a small compromise seemed impossible.

I received a phone call one day early in the pandemic from a family member asking if I was going to wear a mask. I said I was, and hoped for the betterment of mankind everyone, worldwide, would also. They felt this COVID virus was just a hoax. I had heard that, but people were dying, I told this family member, some were our friends, so to be on the safe side, "let's all just wear a mask when out in public." I couldn't see how this was too much to ask. To me it boiled down to two things: we either put the well-being of others first, or our own selfish desires. My fear was contracting the virus and passing it on to someone else who later died—I would feel terrible, and, ultimately, responsible for their death. I was willing to wear a mask and social distance as long as it takes to get through this. I felt it was somewhat like being in Vietnam, use good judgment, protect yourself and others and, at some point, my tour and this virus will hopefully become history.

At this very same time our country's political system is going through a bitter conflict. This conflict was affecting everyone in our country and slowly seeping throughout the world. I wish humanity wasn't so selfish and egotistical. We can't seem to live and work together, willing to compromise if needed. I like living in a democracy with sensible laws, but as of now the division between our two political parties are too great to get anything accomplished.

• • •

Now at seventy-five years of age, I would guess I'm about 80 percent through my time here on earth. I'm physically and mentally slowing down, but I still want to be productive and contribute to society. At this point I have two interests, writing and woodworking. If my writing could inspire or encourage even a few folks, I would be pleased. If a small woodworking project could be a pleasing gift to not only friends but also to strangers, I would also be pleased. I don't know how much time I have left but I hope to use that time to give back to humanity. That would be a fulfilling way to come to the end of my block of time.

Epilogue

It's a beautiful spring morning, low humidity, mild temperature. I'm sitting in an old, yet comfortable, wooden rocking chair on the porch of my woodworking shop. In the dense woods, I hear the beautiful sound of a wood thrush. I always welcome their return in the spring.

This morning my soul is at peace. I rarely have this peace, so when I do, I savor it. Our two dogs, Molly and Maggie, and our cat, Bugs, are lying on the porch sleeping, enjoying the warm rays of the sun on their shiny coats. Just having loyal loving pets adds to my contentment. I can't elaborate enough on this peace and contentment. I feel it's even more appreciated after a lifetime of heartache, pain, and injustice.

At these times, I seem to ponder or think my best. This morning, I find myself not reflecting on my good or bad decisions—that's history now and can't be undone. I now wonder what's in store after I die. Will I get to meet my Uncle Bill and Roy? My grandmother and parents? My wife, Kimball? Or the young Vietnamese girl? How about Rocky and Maggie, my loyal loving cat and dog? How about God? And will He be available for conversation. Or will I just decompose to a handful of dust?

I certainly don't know how much longer I'll be alive; I don't feel I'll live the length of time my mother and father did. I don't have any misgivings how my life turned out, at least so far. My actions, the good and the bad, have shaped who I've become, yet it's just natural for me to continue to wonder or ponder life until my last breath.

Acknowledgements

I want to say thank you to everyone I mentioned and all those who were on the scene but didn't. All of you have had an impact on my life.

I want to also thank my dear friend Christian Lau for reading a rough draft of the military portion many years ago. His insight and suggestions were truly appreciated and opened up a deeper understanding of my military experiences.

John Lee, I refer to him as my shrink, because he worked as a Rehabilitation Counselor for the state of Tennessee, also reviewed the manuscript, encouraged me and added suggestions. I'm thankful to have John and Christian, two godly and spiritually minded men in my life.

Sayde Walker, project manager for Launch My Book Inc, took me by the hand and patiently guided me through the process of publishing. Her calming demeanor and professionalism made her a joy to talk and correspond with. I always felt I was in good hands.

Laura Didyk, who had the daunting task of editing, was simply outstanding. Reading her work was amazing, what was rough and jumbled was now smooth and flowing. She was able to get into my mind, to understand where I was coming from, what I was trying to say.

Jeanne Schmitzer, my wife, has always encouraged me to write. I'm fortunate to have her as my partner in life.

About the Author

Bill lives in rural Tennessee with his wife, Jeanne. In his free time he enjoys woodworking.